# HANNAH & FRIENDS

*Life in South Brisbane*
*1843 – 1870*

**BRIAN HANSFORD**

Inspire Point
PUBLISHING

Copyright © Brian Hansford 2022

All rights reserved. No part of this book may be reproduced by any means, except where permitted under the Copyright Act, without the written permission of the publisher.

Inspire Point Publishing
PO Box 972
Beenleigh, Queensland 4207
Australia
Email: admin@inspirepointpublishing.com

 A catalogue record for this book is available from the National Library of Australia

Designed by Peta Hansford

Hannah & Friends: Life in South Brisbane 1843-1870
ISBN: 978-0-6482981-4-4

## Table of Contents

Acknowledgments vii
Illustrations x

### Part 1 – Hannah in South Brisbane

Incredible Women 3
Snapshot of Hannah 7
Hannah Sweeny 9
Andrew Graham 13
Thomas Graham 16
Andrew Marries Hannah 19
Andrew and South Brisbane Allotments 23
Hannah Graham 30
Harp of Erin and George Croft 35
Andrew and Labour Shortage 38
Andrew's Involvements 44
The Role of Inns 48
Andrew and Shipping Intelligence 50

| | |
|---|---|
| Conditions in Brisbane | 56 |
| Death of Andrew | 60 |
| Inventory at Harp of Erin | 62 |
| Andrew's Will | 65 |
| Hannah Takes Over | 73 |
| Hannah and Frank Mercer | 76 |
| Frank Mercer v's Arthur Lyon | 85 |
| Bush Inn and the Mercers | 87 |
| Frank Mercer and Champoo | 90 |
| Frank Mercer and Horses | 92 |
| Frank: Insolvency and Death | 94 |
| Hannah and Genteel Board | 96 |
| Hannah and 1860 Court Cases | 100 |
| Hannah Moves to Ipswich | 103 |
| Hannah's Death | 105 |
| Supreme Court and Hannah's Children | 111 |
| Reflecting on Hannah and Friends | 115 |
| Final Snapshot of Hannah | 131 |
| Hannah's Timeline | 134 |

## Part 2 – Hannah and her Neighbours

| | |
|---|---|
| Background | 139 |
| Lot 1 Elizabeth Connolly | 145 |
| Lot 5 Section 6 Elizabeth Connolly | 159 |
| Lot 2 Andrew Graham | 163 |
| Lot 3 William Sheehan | 171 |
| Lot 4 William Lacy | 184 |
| Lot 5 John Orr | 187 |
| Hannah and the Allotments | 189 |
| Overview | 191 |
| Conclusions and Hannah's Views | 198 |
| Endnotes | 206 |
| Index of People | 210 |

## Acknowledgments

Over the last 15 years, I have spent a considerable proportion of my time collecting and organising material about early settlers in what is now called South East Queensland. In 2016, *The Elusive Archibald Young* was published. The major considerations in this book were the years Young spent as a farmer at Ipswich and then in the management of the Samford Run. *William Jubb* (2018) was at Allora as a blacksmith and as an innkeeper at the *Woolpack Inn*, Cunninghams Gap. The current book, *Hannah and Friends*, has as its focus a young Irish woman, Hannah Sweeny, who became an innkeeper in South Brisbane, Kangaroo Point and Ipswich.

Archibald Young, William Jubb and Hannah Sweeny are virtually unknown figures in the early colonial settlements. They are best described as 'everyday people' or 'small cogs'. On a remote and isolated large island, it was the many 'small cogs' that held the settlements together.

The current book is in two parts. The first part, *Hannah in South Brisbane*, describes her working life in South Brisbane, Moreton Bay District. The second part,

*Hannah and her Neighbours*, discusses her neighbours and to whom they sold their allotments.

I am fortunate that my wife Jean tolerates my comments and questions about Hannah. At times I suspect she wonders to herself, 'who on earth is Hannah?' Thank you Jean for just being you.

Russell Black, a great-great-grandson of Hannah, has been extremely helpful in the development of the first part of this book. He is fascinated with his family's history, and building on the work of his aunties and other relatives has collected many names, dates and facts to build their family genealogy. I had been working on this book for some time when I located the genealogical work of Russell and other family members. This family is extremely proud of their ancestor, Hannah. Russell, who works in Brisbane, now walks in the footsteps of his great-great-grandmother, Hannah.

Thank you to Kaye Nardella, Senior Curator of the Museum of Natural Resources, Mapping and Environment, for your assistance with the application *QImagery*, advice regarding the accessing of title deeds and the ownership of allotments by William Sheehan.

Peta Hansford of Inspire Point Publishing, Beenleigh, has been a marvellous support for this book. She has designed and set this book up, including the placement of illustrative materials. There is no way this author could self-publish a book. Peta's technical knowledge and common sense have saved me from falling over the edge. Thank you again, Peta.

Barry Shaw, a member of the Brisbane History Group, has been an excellent sounding board at coffee meetings. He also located various relevant references in early Brisbane History Group publications and made many constructive comments regarding the text.

Darcy Edwards, whose great-great-grandfather James Reid, lived on the other side of Stanley Street, a very short distance from Andrew and Hannah Graham's inn, has provided valuable knowledge regarding this area of Brisbane.

The volunteers from the various historical groups deserve great praise for the work they do ensuring local history is retained. With regard to this book, I thank the Raymond Terrace Historical Society for their advice concerning the Graham family, the Coonabarabran Historical Group Inc for their comments relating to Ebenezer Orr and the Logan River Family History Society Inc for information relating to the Logan Hotel and settlers on the Logan River.

The second part of this book is based on legal documents. Paul Sayer, a consultant for *Queensland Law Group*, translated some legal terms for me. He also spent considerable time explaining a legal document relating to Section 3 Allotment 3. Thank you for your kindness, Paul.

I hope those who read this book gain a degree of appreciation and enjoyment.

# Illustrations

## Part 1

1. *Brisbane (from South Brisbane)*, Engraver: J C Armytage, circa 1874, (cover).

2. Excerpt from lithograph of *Brisbane*, 1888, Artist: W A Clarson, *Supplement to the Illustrated Sydney News*, 30 August 1888. Part 1 title page illustration showing Hannah's inn on bottom left-hand side.

3. Baptism record for Hannah Sweeny, 1825, (http://www.ancestry.com) Ireland Births and Baptisms, 1620–1911.

4. Marriage record of Hannah Sweeney and Andrew Graham, 1845, Roman Catholic Marriages Parish of Brisbane, County of Stanley.

5. Allotments purchased by A Graham in South Brisbane, *Ham's Map of the City of Brisbane* 1863, Department of Natural Resources and Mapping.

6. Lithograph of *Brisbane*, 1888, Artist: W A Clarson, *Supplement to the Illustrated Sydney*

News, 30 August 1888 and *Ham's Map of the City of Brisbane,* 1863, Department of Natural Resources and Mapping, showing Stanley Street location of Hannah's inn (*Pride of Erin/Steam Packet Hotel*).

7. Photograph of Dr Kevin Izod ODoherty, Source: State Library of Queensland Document Supply, 110815.tif (4/5/2021)

## Part 2

8. *Ham's Map of the City of Brisbane* 1863 showing Hannah's neighbours at allotments 1 to 5 in Section 3, and allotment 5, Section 6, South Brisbane, Department of Natural Resources and Mapping (also used as background image Part 2 title page).

9. Portrait of Robert Towns (1860s), Source: Queensland State Archives (19/4/2021). Name of artist and year of production not known.

10. Statue of Robert Towns, Source: Diane Watson, Monument Australia Coordinator (15/4/2021).

11. Portrait of Jacob Montefiore, J.P, FRGS, 1885, Artist: Barnett Samuel Marks. Source: State Library of South Australia. No known copyright restrictions for photograph (B9394) (12/4/2021)

12. Photo of *St Patricks Tavern*, Brisbane ca 1873, Source: Queensland University of Technology, Digital Collection, Sub Collection of Robert Augustus Henry L'Estrange.

13. Legal Schedule for Lot 3 (William Sheehan), Source: Title Deeds relating to Lot 3 Section 3 from the Department of Natural Resouces, Mines and Energy.

14. Photograph of Suzie Wong's Good Time Bar, 678 Ann Street, Fortitude Valley (2021), Google maps, edited P Hansford.

15. Photograph of Alfred Shaw & Co display tent at International Exhibition 1876, Source: Alfred Shaw & Co in Queensland (1876) and www. beresford./org./history/ images/ Shaw Ekka 460145 jpg.

16. Table of allotment owners, Lot 1-5 Section 3, South Brisbane, 1843–1887.

17. Aerial photograph of South Brisbane showing lots owned by A Graham, Source: Google maps, 2019.

# Part 1
# Hannah in South Brisbane

2. Part 1 title page illustration is excerpt from a lithograph of *Brisbane*, 1888, showing Hannah's inn on Stanley Street, South Brisbane, in the bottom left-hand corner.

## Incredible Women

There were women who arrived in the early years of the NSW colony who had status or rank that arose from the male members in their family or group having money and contacts. For example, three sisters from the Macarthur family in Sydney made what would be considered 'good' marriages. Two of the sisters married members of the influential Leslie family from the Darling Downs. The other sister married John Clements Wickham, who retired after a distinguished career in the Royal Navy as Captain and was then appointed Police Magistrate and later Government Resident of Moreton Bay District.

Much has been written about the women in the Macarthur, Leslie and Wickham families. These families also wrote letters to relatives in the United Kingdom, the Colonial Secretary and other important administrative persons. There were also substantial diary entries recorded.

Hannah Sweeny, an 18-year-old Irish girl, who arriving in Brisbane in 1842 had no such links. No evidence was located that she ever contacted Ireland again. It seems reasonable to say that Hannah was an example of those women who arrived in the remote colony lacking in resources and a support network. These women were quite different from the wives and daughters of what could be called the colonial aristocracy who had access to means and influential associates.

Looking for an appropriate term to describe these women is difficult. Such terms tend to pigeon-hole the group and conjure up an image of sameness. There was, of course, variability in terms of their age, origins, experience, education and desire to move ahead. The sameness was that they were women who had, for a range of reasons, left their country of origin. Many of these women must have known well the emotions of grief, fear, depression and insecurity. On arriving in towns such as Brisbane and Ipswich in the 1840s, they did not see Utopia, but rather small, grubby, smelly, isolated and potentially dangerous villages. They probably considered they were near the edge of the known world.

The expression 'invisible women' had considerable appeal, but as always, it depends on how the expression is defined. Caroline Perez (2019)[1] used the term 'invisible women', but her term was defined in a way that implied strong political links relating to the deliberate and discriminatory endeavour to distort information. This term is too modern to use with regard to those women arriving in the mid-1800s. The terms 'ordinary' or 'working' women seemed possibilities, but both had a rather belittling connotation. Perhaps 'incredible' is a good expression to use. These women survived in a raw and challenging environment where there was a critical shortage of women. As in their home countries, there was a male dominance in society.

These incredible women were the wives of shepherds and labourers on large runs. They were the housekeepers, cleaners, cooks, maids, servants, dressmakers, barmaids and shop assistants. Many of these women lived in remote and sometime dangerous locations. In some instances, these women did not have other women to talk to. Medical assistance or advice could be hundreds of kilometres away. Their friends and relatives were thousands of kilometres away in United Kingdom. Quite a number were illiterate, and some had survived their early years as convicts.

There was a shortage of positions where these women could become employed and earn enough to hold their lives together: some of these incredible women became prostitutes.

The initial objective of this book was to identify a group of ten or so incredible women and write a book about their lives. It took a few weeks to realise that this was well beyond the scope of an unfunded project.

There was also the fact that an examination of the early colonial newspapers confirmed something I was probably already aware of, but had not realised the immense significance of. These newspapers were largely run by men and were, to a considerable extent, about men. Women were the necessary goods and chattels for successful men, and although a number of these incredible women were mentioned in early colonial newspapers, they were generally not discussed in any real depth.

Brian Hansford

It is highly likely that the early incredible women, who upon arrival in the Moreton Bay and Darling Downs districts, questioned their capacity to make a go of living in this rather strange land. Many did, and are now the building blocks of incredible Australian family trees.

## *Snapshot of Hannah*

This is the story of a young Irish girl named Hannah Sweeny who was born in Cork in 1825, and in the same year was baptised as a Roman Catholic in Killarney, Ireland.

Hannah was probably one of the many Irish people who left their homeland as a result of the appalling conditions leading up to the Great Potato Famine. Her destination was the colony of New South Wales (NSW). Hannah sailed on the *Susan* and arrived in the colony on 25 March 1841. Documentation shows that there were immigrants from Scotland, England and Ireland travelling on the *Susan*. Thirteen of the Irish immigrants were from the County Cork, and one of these was Hannah.

When Hannah arrived in Brisbane in 1842, she was 18 years old. The convict settlement had been closed since 1839, and this meant a reasonable proportion of the population of Brisbane had been relocated. From 1842, land was opened to new settlers and the rather grubby face of a town called Brisbane began to change.

Hannah became Hannah Graham when she married Andrew in 1845. He was a young man on the go with a number of business interests, including the ownership of an inn. Following Andrew's death, she married Frank in 1851 and became Hannah Mercer. Frank was described as a sportsman who had interests in boxing and horse racing but also became involved with inns. Hannah died in late 1862 at Ipswich, where she held an innkeeper's licence.

**Hannah Sweeny**
in the **Ireland, Select Births and Baptisms, 1620-1911**

| | |
|---:|:---|
| Name: | Hannah Sweeny |
| Gender: | Female |
| Baptism Date: | 15 May 1825 |
| Baptism Place: | Roman Catholic, Killarney, Kerry, Ireland |
| Father: | Edmund Sweeny |
| Mother: | Mary Connor |
| FHL Film Number: | 823809 |

Source Information
Ancestry.com. *Ireland, Select Births and Baptisms, 1620-1911* [database on-line]. Provo, UT: Ancestry.com Operations, Inc., 2011.
Original data: *Ireland Births and Baptisms, 1620-1911*. Index. Salt Lake City, Utah: Family Search.

3. Baptism record of Hannah Sweeny, 1825

## Hannah Sweeny

It was when writing previous books about Archibald Young and William Jubb, two early settlers in the northern districts of the colony of NSW, that I first saw mention of Hannah in a newspaper.[2] This mention was of Hannah Mercer in an 1855 issue of the *Moreton Bay Courier*.[3]

In April 1855 Margaret Jubb became critically ill and William, the then innkeeper of the *Woolpack Inn*, Cunninghams Gap, decided to take his wife to Ipswich and then on to Brisbane by steamer for medical treatment. The Mercers were running what was initially called *Young's Bush Inn*. Margaret Jubb was attended by Hannah Mercer during their trip towards Ipswich. As the Jubbs crossed the Fassifern Valley in pouring rain, their dray hit a stump, tipped over and Margaret was killed. Jubb, in a letter published in the *Moreton Bay Courier*, thanked Hannah Mercer for her kindness during this tragic trip.

As mentioned, Hannah would have left Ireland just as the country was about to head into the Great Potato Famine. This famine arose from an interaction of several factors. The two major factors being the outbreak of the disease known as potato blight and a legal system heavily biased in favour of absentee English landlords. Food became extremely scarce, virtually no jobs were available and living conditions were grim.

Records tell of the departure of large numbers of Irish people prior to the major impact of the famine. Rushen in *Colonial Duchesses* (2014) presents information about 750 free, single and carefully selected Irish women who were brought to the colony of NSW between 1835 and 1836.[4] Rushen argues that many of these women established successful lives. Much of the literature tends to present a rather different view of the Irish women who emigrated to NSW. They were often depicted as licentious, troublesome, and many were the products of poverty, disease and hopelessness.

The Irish departures were not just to NSW. Between 1823 and 1825, Peter Robinson, a Canadian soldier, fur trader and politician, organised the movement and settlement of 2500 poor Catholic families from the area around Cork to the Ottawa Valley in Canada.

Hannah Sweeny left Ireland in 1840, as did Andrew Graham and Catherine Knox. They were heading to Brisbane, and at that time probably had little idea of the disaster that was to occur in their homeland. The reports and letters written during the famine are vivid and distressing. The brutality of the famine years in Cork is discussed on the website *www.irishexaminer.com* in the following manner:

(There was) one mass of famine, disease and death… the dead were wrapped in calico bags and conveyed to the church yard in a reusable coffin… known as a "trap" or "sliding coffin". This reusable coffin had a hinged bottom trapdoor. (Comments were also made about) the defilement and dismemberment of unburied bodies by vermin and dogs … (and the) total apathy and singular indifference with which death was regarded.

When Hannah arrived in the Moreton Bay District in 1842, the town at which she disembarked was divided by the Brisbane River, and the expressions 'north' and 'south Brisbane' were already in use. Hannah took up residence in South Brisbane where the population may have reached a few hundred. The climate, terrain, vegetation and animal life were entirely different from what she experienced in Ireland. The cooler month temperatures in Brisbane were similar to the summer temperatures Hannah had experienced in Cork. It is likely that the vastly different environment Hannah found herself in were simply background factors. Her immediate focus was on existence. How could she exist in this remote, isolated and largely British outpost?

From the late 1830s into the 1850s, there was a shortage of labour in the Moreton Bay and Darling Downs districts. The 1839 removal of convict labour from the northern pastoral areas and the small towns such as Ipswich and Brisbane resulted in a significant decline of a cheap labour force. Various assisted passage schemes focussed on young women, domestic servants and agricultural labourers. The selection of suitable assisted passage personnel was strongly biased toward Southern Ireland. Hannah, living in Cork, certainly fitted the requirements of being from Southern Ireland. She may not have been one of the carefully selected emigrants, but she was resourceful and at a young age gained recognition in the Moreton Bay District.

The combination of famine in Ireland and assisted passage schemes saw an immense decrease in the Irish population. Many different figures are quoted regarding this population decrease, and it is conservatively placed at approximately 1.5 to 2 million people between 1841 and 1850.

# Andrew Graham

To gain a greater understanding of the life of Hannah Sweeny (Graham), it is necessary to consider Andrew Graham's initial marriage to Catherine Knox. Graham was from Magilligan, Londonderry. Andrew's father, also called Andrew Graham, and his uncle Richard Graham had both been officers in the 37th Foot Regiment.

Prior to leaving Ireland, Andrew stayed with his uncle Reverend John Graham (1774–1844), quite a divisive figure in Ireland's history. Although born a Roman Catholic, he recanted and became the rector of Tamlaght and Magilligan from 1824 to 1844. Some sources suggest he also lived at Ballymahon and that family members were buried there. It is also known that he lived in Derry for a period of his life. Graham became a trenchant critic of Catholicism and wrote many poems relating to historic Irish incidents that incorporated his religious stance. He participated in a sectarian riot and was imprisoned. To some, he was 'the poet of the Orangemen' and to others, 'crazy Graham' writing doggerel. It would have been surprising if the views of Reverend Graham did not have some impact on the young Andrew Graham.

In 1840 Andrew Graham boarded the *Lord Western* with his wife Catherine Knox from Kilkenny. They were heading to the British colony of NSW as assisted immigrants. These Irish immigrants received a combined sum of £36/3/6 for their decision to journey to NSW. The shipping list from the *Lord Western* and allied documents indicated that the Grahams were Protestants. Andrew was described as a farm labourer who could read and write, and Catherine as a farm servant who could read. The Grahams made their way to Newcastle (NSW) and the river port towns of the lower Hunter River.

Thomas Graham, a cousin, placed a notice in the *Sydney Monitor and Commercial Advertiser,* August 1841, for Andrew to contact him via the Post Office, Newcastle. This advertisement read:

**Mr. Thomas Graham**

SON to the Rev. John Graham of Magilligan Glebe, county Londonderry, will hear of his cousin, Mr. Andrew Graham, who arrived in the ship Lord Western in October. Address if by letter, Post Office, Newcastle.

The notion that Andrew Graham and Catherine Knox married before they became assisted immigrants in 1840 was a clever but illegal ruse, as young married couples received more financial assistance than single immigrants. Their official marriage was celebrated in September 1841 at Raymond Terrace, Newcastle. They had one daughter, Ann, and there is some doubt surrounding the date Ann was born. Apparently

Catherine was 20, and the birth took place at Morpeth, which is approximately 17 kilometres from Raymond Terrace. Ann may have been born before the Raymond Terrace wedding. This would have been of little concern to a young, impetuous man like Andrew Graham.

## Thomas Graham

We know that Andrew made his way to the Newcastle area and that Thomas Graham advised him in August 1841 to make contact via the Newcastle Post Office. In September 1841 Andrew married Catherine in a Catholic ceremony at Raymond Terrace, and in the same year they had a daughter, Ann, at Morpeth. Catherine was a Catholic, despite the claim of being a Protestant in the shipping records of the *Lord Western*.

Relatives of Hannah in Brisbane believe it is possible that Thomas Graham came out to NSW to attend the wedding of Andrew and Catherine. The other possibility was that Thomas was living in the region near Newcastle and a search was conducted to see if this possibility could be validated.

When certain names arise during a search, a great number of results can be produced; Graham is such a name. Searching in the Newcastle and Lower Hunter River areas resulted in many 'hits' on a man called George Thomas Graham. This Graham received a 640 acre land grant from Governor Ralph Darling near Raymond Terrace in 1827. He had worked for the Australian Agricultural Company (AAC) for some years and had reached the rank of superintendent. His history was not an appropriate fit for the Thomas Graham that Andrew was seeking.[5]

The *Raymond Terrace Historical Society* (*Personal Communication*, 21 March 2019) reported that G T Graham was English, thus ruling out a possible link to Andrew Graham. It was also stated by the *Raymond Terrace Historical Society* that there had been a man called Thomas Graham who had operated the punt (ferry) at Hinton approximately four to five kilometres from Morpeth for a number of years. This Thomas Graham had donated to the appeal for the poor Irish and may well have been Irish himself. *The Sydney Morning Herald* in December 1839 reported that a ferry was operating at Hinton that year. By 15 January 1842 the *Hunter River Gazette* reported that Thomas Graham of 'the Punt, Hinton' had two boats for sale. This Graham also did not fit the profile of Andrew's relative.

There was another view about Thomas Graham based on a belief that Thomas Graham came out from Ireland for the 1841 wedding. Russell Black, a great-great-grandson of Hannah Graham (nee Sweeny) (R W Black *Personal Communication* 16 March 2019) expressed a view that as Andrew was a Protestant and Catherine a Roman Catholic, such mixed marriages required permission. Black suggested that this permission may have been arranged in Ireland and travelled to the colony with Thomas.

The need for approval in mixed religion marriages existed at that time. To get the greatest financial advantage possible from an assisted passage to NSW Andrew and Catherine made certain claims. They said they were both Protestants and married. Neither claim was true. There may be queries concerning their integrity, but this does not preclude religious fervour from determining which church they would be married in.

In May 1842 Andrew placed a notice in the *Sydney Morning Herald* for the attention of his cousin William Graham, Esq., Surgeon R N. It seems that William was to arrive in the colony soon. Andrew pointed out that 'in a few days' he was 'about to proceed to England'. Early steam ships took between 80 to 90 days to make such a trip and thus Andrew would have been out of the colony for well over 6 months. The purpose of this trip is not known, but two possibilities exist. Andrew had strong links to UK family members, and it may have been just a trip to reinforce these ties. He was also involved in exploring the financial possibilities of providing labourers for the many positions available in the colony of NSW.

To make this trip, Andrew was leaving his young wife Catherine with a baby who was not yet one-year-old. In retrospect, it must be remembered that the male dominated society simply anticipated that women would have babies and look after them.

## *Andrew Marries Hannah*

Life for a young Irish woman living in South Brisbane must have been rather complex in the mid-1840s. There was a small population of around 300, most of whom were male. Some of these men were ex-convicts, and the remainder were largely from the UK. The families of a number of these departing males from the UK probably gave a large sigh of relief as they left their homeland for some distant land called New South Wales. Despite their origins and reasons for departure, these new male settlers had an interest in common—women. Hannah probably spent a proportion of her time as what can best be described as 'on guard'.

There was a census conducted in NSW in 1841, and this emphasised the gender disparity confronting Hannah on her arrival in Brisbane. In the total Moreton Bay District, there were 2,082 males and 105 females. Fifty-six of these females were married. Hannah probably spent not a proportion of her time 'on guard', but most of her time.

Unfortunately, Andrew Graham's wife Catherine died on 5 January 1845. He now had an inn and a young daughter to look after. There were also other business interests he was endeavouring to establish.

Less than three months after the death of Catherine, Andrew Alexander Hamilton Graham, the licensee of the *Harp of Erin* inn, married the 20-year-old Hannah Sweeny on the 25 March 1845.

It may be unfair or uncharitable to suggest that one of Graham's motives in marrying Hannah so soon after Catherine's death was that he now had someone to look after his little daughter Ann. Another possibility was that he was completely infatuated by a breathtakingly beautiful 20-year-old Irish woman.

The marriage certificate reveals nothing about the role played by love, lust or convenience, but it does provide historical information. Despite Andrew's contact with his uncle, Reverend John Graham, and his aggressive anti-Catholic poetry, he once again took a Catholic bride and was married by a Catholic priest, Reverend James Hanly. The aggressive religious views Graham had been exposed to in Ireland appear to have had little impact on his marriage decisions in colonial NSW.

Hanly was the first permanent Catholic priest in Brisbane. To be a successful cleric in the 1840s and 1850s, it was necessary to travel miles to meet your parishioners. Hanly apparently was a good horseman and kept several horses in Boundary Street, Brisbane, at a property called *Castleracket*. The Brisbane heritage documents relating to St James College report that in 1852 Hanly paid £30/5/8 for just over 3 acres in

Boundary Street. He certainly rode many miles, and on one occasion was well south in the New England district.

4. Marriage record of Anne (Hannah) Sweeney and Andrew Graham 1845

When Hannah Sweeny married Andrew Graham, the marriage certificate identified her as Anne Sweeney. Russell Black, in various emails to the author, noted that Hannah could be called Hanna, Anna, or Joanna. This apparently was not a problem. Similarly, the change in the spelling of her surname from Sweeny to Sweeney was probably viewed as a trivial matter.

The witnesses to the marriage were William Fitzpatrick and his wife Mary Anne, who signed with an 'X'. This was not unusual as the census data for Stanley County in 1846 reported that in excess of 50% of the adults in the county were illiterate. It is noted that four years after Hannah's marriage to Graham, she requested that Fitzpatrick be one of the persons appointed to review the debts of the *Harp of Erin* inn.

During the first months of his appointment as police magistrate in 1843, Captain Wickham named William Fitzpatrick as Chief Constable, a position he held until 1850. Fitzpatrick had previously been Assistant Superintendent in Sydney. A map entitled *Brisbane and Suburbs: According to Original Crown Grants* (1900) shows that Fitzpatrick obtained nearly 23 acres of land. Four allotments were between Montague Road and the Brisbane River, and three adjoining allotments on the other side of Montague Road.

When Wickham appointed Fitzpatrick, he also appointed four other constables and the administrative requirements that followed were excruciating. Names had to be forwarded to Sydney and also their recommended salaries. Fitzpatrick received £4 per month. Pistols and muskets had to be requested. Eighty pistol balls and 80 musket balls were ordered. The multitude of requests from the Moreton Bay District to Sydney must have been an organisational nightmare for the relationship between the two locations.

## Andrew and South Brisbane Allotments

The first allotments of Brisbane land went up for sale in Sydney on the 14 July 1842. *The Sydney Gazette and New South Wales Advertiser* in July 1842 was unimpressed with some of the South Brisbane allotments as they were situated in close proximity to a swamp which overflowed daily at high water.

In the 1840s Graham purchased two allotments in South Brisbane. The first was Allotment 3 Section 4 in Grey Street, South Brisbane. Although the freehold title was not granted until 1844, he obtained a licence for the *Harp of Erin* inn on 13 June 1843. Graham's second purchase was in August 1847 of Allotment 2 Section 4 in Stanley Street, South Brisbane. At various times both sites were used for the operation of the *Harp of Erin* inn.

There were five adjoining allotments on the north side of Stanley Street where Graham had made his purchase. The price for each of these was as follows:

| | |
|---|---|
| Elizabeth Connolly | £22/19/- |
| Andrew Graham | £29/14/- |
| William Sheehan | £26/02/- |
| William Lacy | £22/10/- |
| John Orr | £22/10/- |

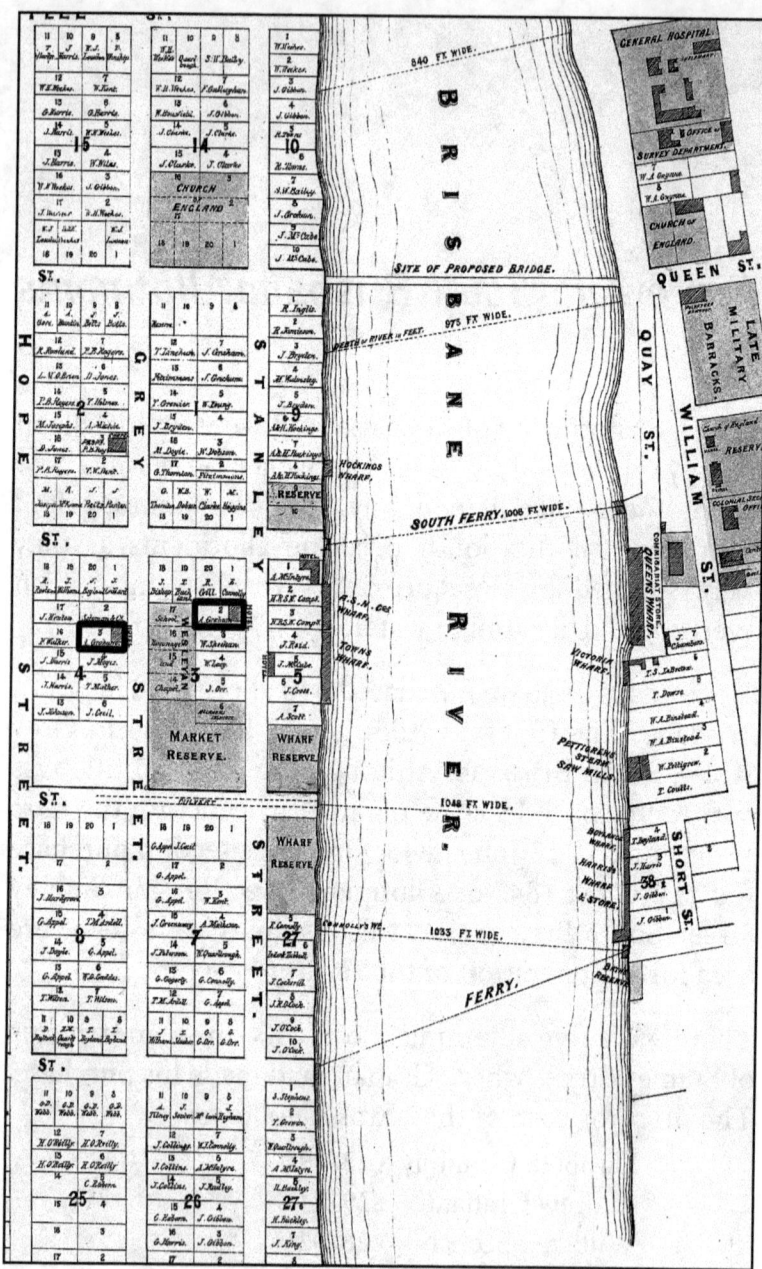

5. Allotments purchased by Andrew Graham

The fact that Graham paid the highest price probably had nothing to do with soil fertility or the commanding view of the area. It may have been the least affected by tides, nearby swamps, streams and floods.

On 10 December 1921 the *Brisbane Courier* reported a talk given by Frank Cumbrae-Stewart from the then History Society of Queensland to members of the United Licensed Victuallers Association. This presentation was entitled *'Inns and Roads of Moreton Bay'*. Cumbrae-Stewart, a highly respected legal man, became the founding Registrar and Librarian of the University of Queensland. This in-depth presentation suggested that 'A. A. Graham' commenced the *Harp of Erin* inn in 1848 but died in 1849. The date of death was correct, but the inn commenced in 1843.

When the *Harp of Erin* inn began operation in 1843, South Brisbane was a few scattered buildings. Further down the river toward Kangaroo Point was rather undeveloped, and a thick tropical scrub grew along the river.

These two South Brisbane sites remained in the name of Andrew Graham for over 25 years after his death. The Grey Street site sold in 1876 and the Stanley site in 1870. The rent from these sites must have been significant for Hannah, and later her children. If the *Harp of Erin,* Grey Street, is taken as an example, the data in the *Brisbane Hotels and Publicans Index* states that the site was rented by various people. The first seems to have been Hy Tuiss (1850-52), followed by Thomas Hayes (1862-63) and William Lyons (1864-66). No record was located regarding the amount of rent paid for the site. With respect to the *Steam Packet* inn site, the Mercers held the licence from 1848 to 1853. It was then rented by Jas Donald (1853-54), Robert Dix (1854-55), Jos Williams (1855-57) and Francis R Stirling (1857-59).

The *Moreton Bay Courier* on 18 September 1847 expressed deep annoyance about the land sales that had occurred a little earlier in the region. In particular, their irritation was on behalf of Brisbane citizens:

> On Wednesday last another attempt was made to administer the nauseous land pill to the innocent people of Moreton Bay.

The tirade from the paper mainly focussed on the high prices set on the Brisbane allotments compared to those in Ipswich. Considerably more allotments were sold in Ipswich than Brisbane. It was contended that the soil was better at Ipswich and that it only took a few hours more to get to Ipswich by river. The paper claimed that this discrimination against Brisbane had occurred at a time when 'the squatters' were pushing to bypass Brisbane and establish Cleveland as the main port in this northern extension of NSW.

When the newspapers of 1846 reported that Ebenezer Orr made an appearance in the South Brisbane area, it was easy to jump to the conclusion that he may have been a relative of John Orr, the butcher for the Grahams' inn. Ebenezer's name, along with that of his brother James, appeared on the electoral roll for freeholders in South Brisbane. These brothers were probably not related to John Orr.

Ebenezer, or as he was also known, Eban, had a warehouse and dealt in wool. In 1846 the *Moreton Bay Courier* reported that he had five tons of fine flour which was to be sold at public auction by Tom Dowse, the interesting auctioneer who wrote articles under the pseudonym 'Old Tom'. Ebenezer Orr, while at South Brisbane, collected subscriptions for the *Moreton Bay Courier* and was treasurer of the Brisbane Regatta for rowing. Ebenezer, before coming to South Brisbane and after he left, had quite a distinguished historical record in the colony.[6]

The Stanley Street where Graham purchased one of his allotments, is not the Stanley Street that exists today just south of the Brisbane Cricket Ground. In 1842 Henry Wade commenced a survey of Brisbane. A major objective of this survey was to prepare the land for public auction. Stanley Street initially ran past the Vulture Street junction and followed the course of the Brisbane River. It was the street closest to the river and consequently experienced swampiness, one quite deep creek and a few shallow lagoons. The section of Stanley Street between Melbourne and Vulture Street was removed to make room for the World Expo '88 precinct. After Expo '88, this precinct was named South Bank Parklands. The Gallery of Modern Art and South Bank Parklands now cover a good part of the old Stanley Street. The only section of the old Stanley Street is 100 metres running beside the Queensland Maritime Museum.

A project supported by the government and called Queensland Places (*queenslandplaces.com.au*) reported that for a period in the 1840s South Brisbane had 83 houses and North Brisbane 75. In these early years, it seemed likely South Brisbane would become the business section of Brisbane. Floods challenged this possibility, and it was finally the massive 1893 flood that saw the movement of the growing business area to higher ground on the northern side of the river.

There was an interesting comment made in the description of the Queensland Places project regarding building construction in the north and south of the city. Apparently, at one stage in the early years of building construction, 'North Brisbane's were of stone while all but one on the other side was of timber'. In 1841 there was an immense flood in the Brisbane River and its tributaries. The Australian Bureau of Meteorology generated graphs in November 2017 indicating that the 1841 flood level was in fact slightly higher than the legendary 1893 flood level. This data was presented in a document entitled *Known Flood Levels in the Brisbane and Bremer Rivers*. Aspiring South Brisbane businessmen such as Andrew Graham, must have known about this flood. When he built the *Harp of Erin* in 1843, he chose wood rather than stone for the construction.

It is difficult to make an assessment of the financial return from the renting of such properties as those owned by Graham. People advertising houses or rooms for rent in the 1840s and 1850s were disinclined to state a figure for the rent. In 1859 when Hannah advertised a comfortable eleven room house, the advert did state that a careful and permanent tenant might get a reduced rent. Such cautious statements were common with regard to the rate of rent to be paid.

In September 1846 the *Moreton Bay Courier* suggested the rent for a house in Brisbane, suitable for a bank officer, would be around £50 per annum. In the same year, a homeowner who received £20 per annum from rent was granted electoral rights. An advertisement for new cottages in Ipswich stated that a respectable tenant would pay 25 shillings per week, or in other words, £60 per annum. Unskilled labourers had no chance of paying £50 to £60 for rent when they were receiving less than £30 per annum. It was probably a matter of the quality of abode they were seeking. Towns like Brisbane and Ipswich, and some of the grazing runs, had dwellings that could at best be described as 'shacks' or 'shanties'. Such dwellings may not have had floors and the roofing could be rudimentary, but they did the job for those in need.

## Hannah Graham

Hannah lived in South Brisbane and adjoining Kangaroo Point for twenty years, and on the death of Andrew Graham in 1848, she was age 23 and had three sons to look after; John who was born in 1846, Richard in 1847 and Andrew in 1848. It is highly likely that Andrew's daughter Ann was also under the care of Hannah.

The records of *NSW Archives* do not report when Hannah took over the *Harp of Erin* inn, but the *Moreton Bay Courier* makes several references to 'Mrs Graham's public-house' from 1849 and onwards. In a 'raw, rough and tumble' male dominated environment, it was quite an achievement for a 23-year-old woman with three children under four years of age to be running an inn. Andrew's daughter Ann was now eight years old, and it would be no surprise if she played a substantial role in looking after the three young boys.

There was evidence of awareness in many of the historical documents that alcohol was a dire social problem in colonial Australia. Despite this, the magistrates continued to approve an increasing number of liquor licences in the Brisbane, Ipswich and Warwick areas. In 1857 the *Empire* newspaper was critical of the fact that the magistrates had approved 20 licences for the township of Ipswich where the population was just over 2000. There were applications rejected at various licensing meetings and on occasion additional clauses were approved. An example of this took place in 1847 when Graham's *Harp of Erin* was granted approval to remain open until 12.00 midnight. This would have ensured an increased number of 'seedy' people being attracted to this area of South Brisbane.

The unlicensed selling of alcoholic beverages was widespread in the northern districts of NSW. Peter Bennett was one of the well-known sly groggers in South Brisbane. Bennett was arrested and charged with burglary in 1843, but escaped. In July 1846 the *Moreton Bay Courier* expressed their annoyance with the antics of Bennett, who had become a sly grogger. It was claimed that everyone knew, including the constables, that Bennett made nocturnal visits to his supplier in South Brisbane. His customers were the hut-keepers along the Logan and Albert rivers. The newspaper claimed he was making huge profits selling rum at eight shillings and sixpence a quart. Despite the irritation of the newspaper, no evidence of an arrest was noted.

The Temperance Society in Brisbane was quite active in expressing their concern relating to the dangerous outcomes associated with the sale of alcohol. It was believed there was a need to attack the demon rum and that the selling of alcohol to a population containing many ex-convicts could have dangerous and unpredictable outcomes. It is probable that temperance members saw Hannah as a negative influence on the South Brisbane community. Not only did she sell alcohol, but surely the running of an inn was a man's job.

The issue of inequality based on gender remains an ongoing issue 170 years after Hannah Graham made her way around the streets of South Brisbane. At that time women were just another of man's goods and chattels. Letters to the editors of newspapers frequently used the term gentlemen. For example, when William Jubb's first wife was tragically killed, he had a letter published in the *Moreton Bay Courier* thanking people for their sympathy and understanding. One of the people who received special thanks was Hannah Mercer. The commencing salutation and complimentary close of Jubb's letter contained the word 'Gentlemen'. It was almost as if newspapers were for men.

Another example of inequality of the sexes was evidenced when Governor General FitzRoy visited Brisbane in 1854. There was considerable fuss made by the colonial press when the visit was announced: there was to be a 'public function' and invitations were to be sent out. Yes, naturally, women were not invited. It was not just NSW where issues of inequality based on an individual's gender existed. The free settlers and convicts came to NSW with sexual inequality taken as a virtually unquestioned reality. It was what they had experienced all their lives.

Given the nature of licensed inns, it is not surprising that they attracted some of the rough early Moreton Bay citizens.

In 1848 Owen Molloy was hanged for the barbarous murder of John Leonard at Cowpers (Coopers) Plains. Molloy, an Irish convict who had been convicted for seven years on a charge of cow stealing, was transported to NSW in 1832. Molloy and Leonard had been drinking at Hannah Graham's public house prior to Leonard's murder. Molloy was again drinking at Mrs Graham's after the death of Leonard, but this time with John Day, an employee of Graham. Day told Graham that he believed Molloy had murdered Leonard. This frightened Hannah Graham, who asked her employee Day if he could sleep in front of her door. This murder was much publicised as rumours circulated about others being involved in the Leonard murder. Even after Molloy's execution on 18 September 1848 there were claims that he had confessed to other murders.

The relatives of Hannah have long kept information about her and other descendants. It is believed that although the licence for the *Harp of Erin* was in Andrew's name, Hannah had the major responsibility for the running of the South Brisbane inn. (R W Black, *Personal Communication*, 3 November, 2018).

When Hannah held the licence for an inn, members of her family often worked with her. In November 1850 the *Moreton Bay Courier* reported a messy case of theft which occurred on the steamer *Hawk* as it travelled between Brisbane and Ipswich. William Broadhurst was convicted of stealing money and bank orders valued at £6/11/1 from a drunken man identified as James Cash, an early Albany Creek settler. On visiting Mrs Graham's public house, which at that time was the

*Steam Packet Hotel*, Broadhurst unfortunately used one of the bank orders when served by Selina Graham, the niece of Andrew Graham, who was later a witness in the court case.

William Broadhurst was probably well known to authorities in the Moreton Bay courts as a month after the case involving James Cash, he was back in court and fined £2/10/- for drunkenness, obscene language and intemperate conduct in court.

## Harp of Erin and George Croft

One of the first mentions of Andrew Graham at South Brisbane is in *Colonial Secretary Letters*. On 12 December 1842 there is a note regarding A Graham, and a building licence for a house in South Brisbane. This almost certainly refers to the Grey Street allotment purchased by Graham and where the initial *Harp of Erin* was located. Andrew Graham is recorded as holding the licence for the *Harp of Erin Hotel* from 13 June 1843 until the 17 June 1848 and Hannah is mentioned as working in the bar of this hotel.

In 1847-1848 the *Colonial Secretary Letters* contained a request dated 22 March 1847 from George Thorn *Queens Arms Hotel*, Ipswich and Andrew Graham, *Harp of Erin Hotel*, South Brisbane to hold public exhibitions at their hotels. These exhibitions were described as tight and slack rope dancing, horsemanship, and other amusements of the stage. It is not clear if these entertainment extravaganzas went ahead. The link between George Thorn, a dominant figure in the history of early Ipswich, and the Grahams, suggests they had significant contacts within the area. It is uncertain if the above request was in any way linked to the arrival of George Croft in Brisbane.

In June 1847 Andrew Graham placed a notice in the *Moreton Bay Courier* for the attention of George Croft of South Brisbane. Croft was a temporary resident of South Brisbane. He was a showman who had recently performed at the Victoria Theatre, Sydney and previously at Astley's Royal Amphitheatre, London.

John J Knight published 53 articles in the *Queenslander* during 1891-1892 under the heading *The Birth and Growth of Brisbane and Environs*. The *Queenslander* was initially the weekly paper of the *Brisbane Courier*. In one of these articles, Knight stated that the show was held at the New Amphitheatre constructed by Croft. Features included tight rope walking, clowns, recitations, singing, acrobatic feats and fireworks. Initially, things seemed to go well for the Croft entertainment group. Unfortunately, one night an indecent song was included in the repertoire and the *Moreton Bay Courier* took great umbrage and made the following comment:

> The introduction of an obscene song was an outrage without precedent in our experience of public amusement. That this song was encored by part of the audience could be no excuse for the insult offered to the rest … That Mr Croft selected this song to grace the first appearance of his wife, may perhaps demonstrate his own notions of propriety… We would advise him not to suffer such gross impropriety again.

This reported outrage created a drop in attendance and 'the skids were under Croft entertainment'. Brisbane may have been a raw, rough and tumble settlement, but the apparent bastions of decency won the day.

Croft had been staying at the *Harp of Erin* for a few weeks, and both Hannah and Andrew would have known him quite well. He was in debt for board and lodgings amounting to £26/12/3. Unfortunately for Croft, he stored 'scenic effects' at the *Harp of Erin*. Graham stated in a newspaper notice that he would sell 'the goods that belong to Croft, but in my possession', unless the debt was paid within 14 days. According to Knight, this resulted in the end of Brisbane's 'first theatre and its promoter'.

Despite the threats from Graham, Croft apparently did not pay this sizeable debt. As reported later, when Andrew Graham died and a legal dispute arose about his assets, this debt was still active in the accounting records of the *Harp of Erin*; not that the bookkeeping records of the *Harp of Erin* filled you with confidence.

## Andrew and Labour Shortage

The arrival of convicts in Moreton Bay District peaked in 1831 when approximately 1000 repeat offenders arrive in the district. The penal settlement in Brisbane was extremely small when placed beside the figures for the enormous transportation business to Australia. During the transportation years, approximately 164,000 convicts arrived in Australia and 806 ships were involved. When the transportation of convicts to Moreton Bay District ceased in 1839, the colonial papers reported that a dire labour shortage existed.

A lack of capital ensured that the early development of the northern extremities of NSW was indeed slow. The large-scale grazing activities provided the promise of attracting finance to these areas. The closure of the penal colony in Brisbane meant a very cheap labour source had disappeared. Graziers in areas like the Darling Downs made sure their complaints were heard. It was not just the graziers complaining about the lack of labourers. There were a number of exiles being employed in Brisbane and Ipswich as servants or general labourers in the businesses and homes of town dwellers.

Some argued for the recommencement of convict transportation from the United Kingdom. Issues of morality were raised against this suggestion, and some potential employers stated that a considerable number of convicts had been poor employees. It was argued that with regard to becoming shepherds, many convicts had no knowledge of, or desire, to take up such positions. Despite the arguments of morality raised, the cheap labour had advantages for employers. There was also much written in the newspapers about Indian and Chinese labourers being good agricultural workers.

Andrew was often away from the inn as he had many strings to his bow. A check of shipping departures noted Andrew made a number of trips to Sydney. These were most likely associated with his position as an agent to attract suitable workers for the Darling Downs squatters. The *Courier* and the *Queenslander* mentioned that Mr A. Graham 'had been appointed agent for the squatters'. No precise details could be located regarding the conditions of the agreement, when this agency commenced, the amount of money raised by the squatters or how long it lasted. Graham, who arrived as an assisted emigrant, quickly linked the notion of assisted schemes and NSW labour shortages. Given the effort Graham put into this venture, its success clearly meant financial gain to him.

Graham's major activity as an agent was to convince workers who had arrived in Sydney that good positions were available on the Darling Downs, particularly as shepherds. Newspaper reports suggest that the agreement gave Graham access to a labour fund subscribed to by pastoral lessees. The labourers were signed up with some shepherds receiving £25 per annum and hut-keepers £22 per annum. They also received good rations and accommodation. It would be interesting to know what was included in the good rations. Could shepherds occasionally select and eat a lamb? Much of the accommodation for shepherds existed of rudimentary bark huts with dirt floors. These huts would be very chilly in mid-winter on the Darling Downs. There were some settlers on the Darling Downs who considered the wage, rations and accommodation too good a deal for unproven employees.

A considerable amount of comment appeared in newspapers regarding the morality of seeking cheap overseas labourers and which countries could provide the most appropriate workers. John Buckland from Sydney wrote to the editor of the *Moreton Bay Courier* in December 1847 indicating he had extensive knowledge of the natives of India, spoke their language and that he knew where labourers best suited for him and others could be found. Buckland advised others to contact him for additional information.

It was difficult to obtain the type of emigrants suited to the nature of work required on the Darling Downs. The *Moreton Bay Courier* on 12 May 1849 reported that when the *Chaseley*, one of the Dunmore Lang chartered ships, arrived in Brisbane it had a total of 214 persons on board of which 112 were adults. Apparently, many of these adults were accustomed to rather superior working positions. Only ten had been employed to work and these were going to Richard Joseph Smith's boiling down works on the Bremer River. The Smith workers were to be paid £30 per year plus rations. This sounded rather attractive, but this attractiveness was probably diminished when they were informed that they would be working in water all day. The article concluded with this comment:

> At the utmost, there are not more than ten other persons who are likely to engage for bush work.

During 1846 the *Moreton Bay Courier* made several mentions of assisted labourers arriving in the city being tempted to break their agreements and sign other agreements with town businesses or to just loiter around the streets. The *Moreton Bay Courier* was extremely critical of employers who contributed nothing to the labour fund but inappropriately made use of it by poaching workers. The newspaper claimed that Mr Graham had done the right thing, but the poaching of potential labourers created annoyance. For some years there had been tension between the town and the squatters up country and this poaching of workers did nothing to improve this relationship.

The *Moreton Bay Courier* in November 1848, reported an example where Graham collected £14 for the Irish poor from the workers at Fred Bracker's property, *Rosenthal*. Considering Graham lived in South Brisbane, he had travelled over 170 kilometres to *Rosenthal*. He may have ridden all the way or used a well-sprung cart until he reached the ranges leading on to the Darling Downs. Fred Bracker was a successful well-known grazier on the Downs who employed many shepherds. It is hard to believe that the only reason Graham made such a long trip was to collect for the poor. Graham was a businessman and he wanted success. He would have been away for a few days, but he knew Hannah would be looking after the children and running the inn. It is very difficult to assess how successful Graham was in getting shepherds to the squatters on the Darling Downs. Graham met Bracker in November 1848; Graham died the next month.

The colonial newspapers made it clear that the shortage of labour in the grazing areas of the colony produced a problem. Sale of wool meant money would come into the colony and it was much needed for development.

A letter to the editor of the *Moreton Bay Courier* presented a more contentious and troubling view.[7] The writer, describing himself as 'An Englishman', argued that the graziers would make their money and go back to the United Kingdom. It was felt that the labourers would stay on and that the colony would be 'foistered with an inferior race in large numbers'. The writer did not want a mixed population of 'New Caledonians and Coolies from the hills' but rather an 'immigration of white men and Christians' not a 'host of obstinate Heathens'. The roots of the White Australia Policy were well established in the early years of colonial NSW.

When writing the above paragraph, it was impossible not to think about how newspaper editors would handle such a letter today. It would be rejected as press commentators and social media would go into meltdown over such an outrage. At the time, Graham and other employment agents were endeavouring to resolve a problem and make some money. What may have appeared to be a simple objective within human relationships can easily be the cause of varying viewpoints, such as discrimination on the basis of race, jumping out of the woodwork.

## Andrew's Involvements

In the 1840s the *Harp of Erin* was a location where many things happened. It was certainly used for meetings. In August 1848 John Connolly, a Special Bailiff, conducted a sale at the inn of three disputed allotments at Kangaroo Point. The *Argus* in February 1848 mentioned that a noted pugilist 'Paddy Sinclair', the current champion of NSW and known as the Enfield General, had arrived in Brisbane. He had brought with him 'the Belt'. This much vaunted object was to be placed on display at Graham's inn. Paddy Sinclair had a remarkable record as a boxer in England, Van Diemen's Land and NSW. Boxing in the 1840s was a rugged and rather brutal sport, but no record of Paddy Sinclair actually participating in a Brisbane fight during 1848 was located.

Graham spent some time at the *Harp of Erin,* but much of his energy was devoted to the assisted labourer's scheme. He made a number of trips to Sydney; he negotiated on site with some squatters, and a trip to the UK may have been associated with this scheme. Graham also acted as an agent for Cadell's Windsor Ale and for the *Sentinel,* a Sydney newspaper. When a fund was established in Brisbane for the Scottish and Irish Poor, not only did

Graham attend the meeting, he became one of the official collectors.

In November 1847 an employee of Andrew and Hannah Graham at the *Harp of Erin* attempted to burn down the inn. Samuel Davis, described by the *Moreton Bay Courier* as a 'scoundrel', was charged with drunkenness, attempting to start a fire, stealing poultry and destruction of property belonging to his masters, the Grahams. Davis was sentenced to two months hard labour in a Sydney goal. During this incident Andrew Graham went looking for the constables while members of the Orr family from next door kept an eye on Davis.

In December 1847 the *Moreton Bay Courier* reported a case in which Graham laid a charge against a 'vixenish-looking woman' who carried in her arms a small child and was accompanied by a three or four-year-old child. This woman ordered a 'stone-fence', a drink consisting of brandy and ginger ale. She refused to pay and verbally abused both Grahams and struck Hannah. She then went outside and threw stones through the window. A magistrate ruled that she pay a fine of 10/- or in default spend 24 hours in confinement on bread and water. The fine was paid.

When the *Sovereign* sank on the southern end of Moreton Island in March 1847, 44 people lost their lives. Graham's name was among the many prominent Brisbane citizens making a donation to the Sovereign Relief Fund.

An important meeting was held in Brisbane in January 1848 to discuss the location of a Church of England house of worship. Those attending this meeting were significant Church of England citizens: Captain John C Wickham, Dr David Ballow, Robert Little, Reverend John Gregor and Andrew Graham.

The *Shipping Gazette and Sydney General Trade List* of 12 February 1848 reported an A Grahame travelling from Sydney to Moreton Bay. This is almost certainly Andrew Graham of South Brisbane. This A Graham(e) was accompanied by two servants and possibly by a Miss Jessica Orr, a member of the Orr family butchers, who lived just down the road from Andrew and Hannah Graham. Graham died 10 months later from consumption, and it is assumed that the two servants were to help him get around.

In May 1848 a meeting was called to consider an offer made by the NSW government to provide £200 toward the construction of a general hospital in Brisbane. The £200 from the government had to be matched by the Brisbane community. A meeting was called to discuss how the matching funds were to be obtained. This meeting was chaired by Captain Wickham. Although Andrew Graham was not at the meeting, he was placed on the committee, and each committee member was asked to donate £1 to get the fund-raising under way.

As stated earlier, during the 1840s when Andrew and Hannah Graham were running the *Harp of Erin* in Grey Street, the population of Brisbane was very small. It seems that Andrew Graham was well known in Brisbane, and the 'hospital committee' consisted of citizens who were among the founding fathers of Brisbane and Ipswich. Those on the committee were John Richardson, Captain

Richard Coley, Dr Stephen Simpson, Christopher Rolleston, Rev. Benjamin Glennie, Andrew Graham, Francis Bigge, Colin Mackenzie, Richard J Smith, Captain Thomas Collins, Robert Davidson, Daniel Peterson, Walter Gray, John Smith, John Campbell and John Macintyre.

In December 1848 Graham died in Sydney from consumption, a disease now called tuberculous. It is possible that Graham thought treatment for his illness may have been more readily available in Sydney than at the outpost of Brisbane in the 1840s. However, the real business associated with the trip to Sydney was to have his will drawn up.

## *The Role of Inns*

The early inns or hotels such as the *Harp of Erin* were in many ways houses of commerce in the 1840s and 1850s. There was an immense shortage of sterling currency in the colony of NSW, and a barter economy based on such commodities as wheat, spirits, corn and swine flesh developed. There were also 'dump dollars', American dollars, IOUs and bank orders that helped fill the void.

Inns, including the *Harp of Erin*, had to deal with all mediums of exchange. Those inns providing food would have resorted to barter. We can but wonder how many glasses of rum could be obtained for 20 lbs of potatoes or 10 bushels of wheat.

Ward-Brown (1988) in *Rosenthal-Historic Shire* described a case in 1849 of William Jubb, then a blacksmith at Allora on the Darling Downs, selling vegetables to sites as far away as Maryland Run near Stanthorpe. It was not unusual for 'deals' to be arranged. In this case, Jubb received part of the money for the produce and Maryland agreed to pay part of the payment to John Collins, a publican at Warwick. Jubb, who was well versed in the location of inns, was apparently in debt to Collins.

The inns may have been an excellent place to turn your money into water, but they were also significant meeting places. As the new settlers arrived, they used the inns to make contact with people, discuss job possibilities and listen to hair-raising stories from the experienced settlers of what dramas were likely to befall them in the remote areas of the colony.

The contract and seasonal workers, such as shearers, drovers and timber workers, came to the inns 'to let their hair down' and frequently left their money in the care of the innkeepers.

## Andrew and Shipping Intelligence

The inns operating in the Moreton Bay and Darling Downs districts in the 1840s were dependent on Sydney for many of their needs. By 1859 when the new colony of Queensland was approved, a considerable amount of produce still arrived from Sydney.

The following information was obtained from various issues of the *Moreton Bay Courier*. The name of Andrew Graham is used in the heading as he was the named licensee of the inn. This tends to downplay the role played by Hannah at the inn, although the reality was Hannah frequently did the work.

The death of Andrew Graham occurred on 14 December 1848 and from this date Hannah was responsible for the ordering from Sydney and the running of the inn. By 1848 the population of Brisbane was experiencing growth and there were some others named Graham importing from Sydney. For example, a person named Graham imported a bundle of fruit trees from Sydney in January 1850. In April 1852 there was an order for Graham that included 56 bars of iron and 5 drums of oil.

Neither of these orders could be linked to Hannah with any degree of certainty.

There were three orders linked to the name Mrs Graham in 1850, and by the nature of their content, these have been linked to Hannah. These three orders have been added to the list on the following page.

It should be noted that the import data reported below uses the abbreviation 'hhd'. This means hogshead, which is a cask with the capacity to hold 54 gallons (245 litres).

This information does not reflect the entirety of the orders for the *Harp of Erin*. Meat and vegetables would have been sourced locally. Some of the early inns had their own vegetable gardens, and by the 1840s, a few Chinese market gardens had commenced on leased land within 10 kilometres of Brisbane. It is known that there were some vacant blocks around the *Harp of Erin* in the 1840s, and it is possible this potential to produce vegetables was utilised.

Late in 1842 the records of Stephen Simpson, the then Commissioner for Crown Lands in Moreton Bay District, state that he granted two licences for the growing of vegetables in the Brisbane area. These were to Martin Frawley and Thomas Prendergast. Frawley wrote to the editor of the *Morning Chronicle* in 1845 thanking Governor Sir George Gipps for assisting him to change his block in Moreton Bay from a yearly rental to a block that could be purchased. Fisher (2012) suggests that Prendergast was probably the first small-scale farmer at Breakfast Creek. Thomas Dowse, in his writings, praised Prendergast for the wide range and

# IMPORTS FROM SYDNEY FOR ANDREW GRAHAM

| YEAR | DATE | IMPORT SUPPLIES |
|---|---|---|
| 1846 | 8 October | 1 box of candles, 2 cases of gin, 1 qrt cask of brandy, 1 package of bacon. |
|  | 1 November | 1 hhd of rum, 5 cases of gin. |
|  | 26 December | 2 half chests of tea. |
| 1847 | 26 June | 2 barrels. |
|  | 10 July | 9 bags of flour. |
|  | 18 July | 6 bags of flour, 2 bags of salt. |
|  | 22 July | 1 case ? |
|  | 21 August | 2 mattresses, 1 parcel, 1 chest of tea, 4 cases of gin, 2 bags of potatoes. |
|  | 20 November | 2 hhds of ale, 1 bag of potatoes, 1 box ? |
| 1848 | 19 February | 4 chests and 2 x ½ chests of tea, 35 bags of sugar, 5 boxes of salt, 10 bags of flour. |
|  | 4 March | 4 casks of beer, 1 package of boots, 1 bag, 1 box. |
|  | 15 April | 1 hhd of beer. |
|  | 29 April | 18 bags of flour, 6 bags of sugar, 1 package. |
|  | 10 June | 1 hhd of ale, 3 casks, 1 keg of nails, 1 roll of hair. |

|  |  |  |
|---|---|---|
|  | 15 November | 1 bag of flour, 2 bags of potatoes, 3 boxes of cigars, 1 roll of lead, 1 hhd of ale. |
|  | 2 September | ½ case of tea, 1 bag of sugar, 1 hhd of ale, 1 bag of flour, hollands. |
|  | 2 December | 2 chests of tea, 1 keg of tobacco. |
|  | 10 December | 10 chests of tea, 16 cases ? 1 iron chest, 1 packet of cigars, 14 hhds of rum. |
|  | 12 December | 1 hhd of brandy, 1 hhd of ale, 2 casks of cider. |
| 1850 | January | order - 12 cases of gin, 12 cases of bottled beer, 2 cases of 2qrt casks of wine, 2 hhds of rum and a package of tobacco. |

**IMPORTS FROM SYDNEY FOR HANNAH GRAHAM**

|  |  |  |
|---|---|---|
| 1850 | 29 January | 12 cases of gin, 12 casks of bottled beer, 2 cases ? 2 qrt cases of wine, 2 hhds of rum, 2 kegs of nails. |
|  | 23 February | 1 cask of whiting, 1 weighing machine, 6 kegs of wine, 2 kegs of nails. |
|  | 15 November | 5 hhds of beer. |

excellent quality of vegetables he grew on his 50 acre block along the south side at West End. It is quite likely that inns such as the *Harp of Erin* dealt with Frawley and Prendergast.

From 1846 to 1848 the *Harp of Erin* hotel ordered brandy, rum, ale, beer and cider, but based on the orders, it seemed that no wine arrived from Sydney. It was not until January 1850 that the *Harp of Erin* order included 2 cases of 2 quart casks of wine. It is certain that wine was sold at the hotel in 1846, but the source and method of delivery are not known. As Graham was an agent for Thomas Cadell's ale, it was probable that this ale was sold at the *Harp of Erin*.

In June 1848 the *Harp of Erin* order included a keg of nails and in November of the same year a roll of lead appeared on the order. Two kegs of nails were included in each of the orders for January and February 1850. These items suggest some type of building activity. Perhaps this activity was associated with the movement of the operational inn site from Grey to Stanley Street. The June 1848 order also included a roll of hair; probably far too much for repair of a saddle, but more suited for the restuffing of a couch or sofa. The word 'hollands' was noted in a September 1848 order. Hollands gin was initially made in the Netherlands. It was a distilled malted spirit that could be likened to Scotch whisky that had not been aged. Perhaps Graham or some of his customers fancied this drink.

There is simplicity about the orders received from Sydney. Flour, salt, sugar, potatoes and tea are noted in repeat orders. Meat would have been obtained locally, probably from the butcher John Orr who lived quite close to the *Harp of Erin*. A number of meals would have consisted of beef and potato stew, damper and tea. The eating of native animals was quite common, so pigeon pie, kangaroo tail soup and stuffed wombat may well have been the gourmet offerings for overnighters at the *Harp of Erin* inn. It has been suggested that a popular meal for the early European settlers was kangaroo steamer. A kangaroo steamer consisted of finely diced fresh kangaroo and salted pork or bacon packed into a clay pot and steamed in its own juices.

Brisbane and Ipswich were basic, rough and hard drinking towns in the 1840s and 50s. It is virtually impossible to ascertain the volume of liquor consumed at an early inn, although the orders received from Sydney and quoted earlier in this document provide some indication. The Sydney order for 14 hogshead of rum on 10 December 1848 may have reflected some heavy drinkers were expected to have a more than joyful and merry time around Christmas. Given that two days later on 12 December an additional hogshead of rum and a similar amount of ale arrived from Sydney, then heaven knows what happened at the *Harp of Erin* during the 1848 Christmas festivities!

## Conditions in Brisbane

When the Grahams lived in Brisbane, it was a small township on the Brisbane River. It lacked adequate medical facilities and had a very limited business district. A large proportion of virtually everything required to develop Brisbane had to be shipped in from Sydney. This was obviously inconvenient, and it also impacted the cost structures of Brisbane.

In the 1840s and 50s there was a continual problem in areas such as Brisbane as the new arrivals, mainly from Europe, moved into a country with an existing Indigenous population. The Indigenous dwellers resisted the new arrivals and papers such as the *Moreton Bay Courier* contained numerous articles about the near war that occurred between the new arrivals and the original owners of the land. The newspapers produced by Europeans depicted the Indigenous tribes as the troublemakers and made no allowance for the fact that their way of life was basically destroyed. As the new settlers moved into the Northern Districts of NSW, the resentment of their arrival was an issue the Europeans were quickly aware of.

The climatic conditions experienced by the Grahams in the 1840s were similar to those occurring over 170 years later, namely, rather hot and humid summers and a mild winter. Perhaps recent evidence of climate change suggests increased variability now than in the 1840s. Newspapers wrote about the floods in the Stanley, Bremer and Brisbane rivers, and these still remain a dangerous feature of the region. Reports by the Bureau of Meteorology contain comments regarding the immense heights reached by the 1841 and 1893 floods. Many of the settlers buying land in South Brisbane in the early 1840s must have known about the devastation caused by floods. Perhaps two thoughts pushed them on. These were the possibility of economic gain and the opportunistic belief that there would not be another big flood for some years.

The roads in townships such as Brisbane and Ipswich were disgraceful, and roads linking townships were often impassable during the 1840s and 50s. The Limestone road linking Brisbane and Ipswich was more correctly described as a track. Following heavy rainfall, the numerous watercourses entering the main rivers cut the Limestone road in many places. After such heavy rain, people who walked along this road, rode horses, used bullock wagons and drays, or drove stock experienced delays—sometimes for weeks.

A meeting was called at the *Harp of Erin* in 1848 to discuss the problems relating to the Limestone road. It was poorly attended and nothing was resolved. There was substantial ill feeling between 'north' and 'south' Brisbane, and suggestions arose that the meeting was called at the wrong time and at an out of the way location; also there had been inadequate publicity. The road remained a mess for years.

The *Moreton Bay Courier* in March 1848 took a very dim view of the meagre attendance at the above meeting. A vital issue relating to the future development of the area was discussed, and the newspaper mentioned the possibility of self-interest, rivalry and petty causes of disunion being involved.

On 8 August 1850 many of the residents of South Brisbane signed a petition to the Colonial Secretary pointing out that money had been provided for various colonial roads but none for South Brisbane. Hannah was a signatory of this petition. Hannah signed as Hannah E Graham, and as Russell Black pointed out (*Russell Black Email 26/11/2020*) this was the first time it had been noted that Hannah had a second name. A number of the signatories were people who lived near Hannah and were obviously known to her. These included John McCabe, John Orr, William Connolly, William Melville and Thomas Grenier. If roads were improved in the next few years, this was not noted by travellers.

In 1962 an historian, Alan Morrison, delivered a paper about life in Brisbane a hundred years ago.[8] This was a rather speculative paper that highlighted the many problems Brisbane faced. The unwillingness of NSW to take on large development projects in the Moreton and Darling Downs districts meant that when the state of Queensland emerged, the problems were many.

Morrison, drawing upon examples mentioned in the newspapers, noted that there was no real rubbish disposal and that it was tempting to use the river, but this meant that your rubbish became a problem for someone further down the river. Apparently, packs of dogs also roamed the streets day and night and were a danger to man and beast. In terms of poor sanitary conditions, attention was drawn to a Mrs Feeney who did her washing in the water reservoir.

The water supplies received a denouncement from Morrison. It was stated that South Brisbane drew their water from the Woolloongabba swamps and that Brisbane's supply came from a hole in the ground contaminated by animal and vegetable matter. The contents in this hole stewed in the sunshine, and the citizens had to drink this filthy compound.

Morrison reported roads contained ruts, elevations, bogs, pools and quagmires. In some instances, Morrison said distressed and helpless women became bogged in the mud and stood there in a condition of helpless bewilderment.

Thank heavens the 'good old days' have gone.

## Death of Andrew

It was reported earlier that Andrew Graham died of consumption in late 1848 when he was in Sydney on business. There may well be validity in this belief. Upon reading Graham's will, it seems that an important reason for his Sydney visit was to make his will. It is evident he had taken details about who would be the trustees of his final will and testament. He also made an appointment in Sydney to meet with a solicitor and organised for witnesses to be available.

On 10 December 1848 he met with solicitor Nicol Drysdale Stenhouse and witness James Kennedy Montgomery of Sussex Street, Sydney. Stenhouse, a devout Presbyterian and associate of Dunmore Lang, certainly was a solicitor, but his reputation was more as a powerful figure in the colonial literary world.

Montgomery, the witness, is more difficult to pigeonhole. It is extremely likely that Graham was quite ill by 10 December, as he dies on 14 December. One possibility is that Montgomery was the coachman who took Graham to the meeting with the solicitor.

There were other people called James Montgomery in Sydney. For example, there was a ticket of leave granted to a man of this name in 1841. As Graham was quite ill at this time, he may have preferred the witness to be Dr Montgomery, who was described as Surgeon Superintendent.

As Graham's will has a significant effect on Hannah's life, further comment and analysis is found in a following section of this book.

# Inventory at Harp of Erin

Graham held the licence of the *Harp of Erin* inn from 1843 until 1849. There are no known photographs, paintings or sketches of this inn or of Graham. Following Graham's death, a stocktake occurred at the inn in 1850 that provides an inventory of his goods and chattels. This inventory was set out in the following manner:

### *No. 1 Parlour*
One table and cover. Eleven cane bottom chairs. One sofa and cushion.
One couch and cushion. Chiffionier. Book case. Chimney glass.
16 prints and frames. Table lamp. Fender.

### *No. 2 Bedroom*
One bed and bedding. Wash stand and furniture. Chair and glass.

### *No. 3 Middle Parlour*
Two common couches. 12 common chairs. Meat safe.

### *No. 4 Bedroom*
Bed and bedding. Wash stand and furniture. Small table and two broken chairs.

## No. 5 Bar
Four kegs. One filter. One keeler (a shallow tub). Two tin measures. Two tin funnels. Five pewter measures.

## No. 6 Bedroom
Bed and bedding. Small bed and bedding. Wash stand. Chest of drawers. Table. Couch.

## No. 7 Veranda Rooms
One common bed and bedding. Wash stand. One table. Two common couches with cushions. Two tables. One horse hair sofa. 12 cane bottom chairs. Two wash stands. Three iron bedsteads with four mattresses, blankets and sheets.

## No. 9 (No Number 8) Kitchen
One dresser. Two tables. One iron boiler. Copper kettle. One camp oven. Cooking utensils. One iron pot. Four wash tubs. One clothes horse.

## No. 10 Stable
19 empty casks. Horse. Cart and harness.

## No. 11
Stock in trade consisting of spirits, wine and bar glassware. Other things necessary to carry on business.

## Cattle
Yellow poley calf branded PL on side
Yellow poley heifer branded AG on hip and DM on off side hip.
Yellow calf Branded AG on hip.
Horse. (mentioned in No.10).

Looking at the goods and chattels at the inn might suggest the term minimalist was appropriate or 'pretty damn Spartan'. The word 'common' is used several times, whereas we would probably use the words 'plain' or 'simple' to describe particular objects in the inn. When the stable and cattle were mentioned, it is clear that there was a paddock that was used for client's horses. In fact, *Ham's Map of Brisbane* (1863) shows that the land directly behind the allotments of Graham, Sheehan, Lacy and Orr in Stanley Street was designated as a Wesleyan Reserve for a school, parsonage and chapel. For 20 years, this vacant land apparently existed for the use of the residents on the block.

In No. 1 Parlour there is mention of 'chimney glass', which is a dated expression that refers to a mirror placed over a mantlepiece. There was an open fire in this parlour as there is mention of a 'fender' or fire screen to stop sparks or logs from rolling out. A 'chiffionier' was also mentioned as being in this parlour. This is a low cupboard used as a sideboard, or it could have a raised bookshelf on top.

When Grahams purchased meat from John Orr it is assumed that it was put in the meat safe in room No. 3, the middle parlour. In mid-summer this must have been somewhat interesting. Taking a more realistic view, perhaps there was another room where the meat was stored

It was noted that bedroom No. 6 had an adult and a small child's bed in it. Was this room for Hannah to use with her youngest baby? Each bedroom had a washstand, but what about chamber pots? While on this topic, where was the outhouse?

## Andrew's Will

Graham's will is presented on two pages. The following are several of the major points regarding his will.

- The will and probate documents relating to the death of Andrew Graham are quite difficult to read. The writing is small and in the case of the will, 16 words are often crowded to a line. These difficulties are compounded by the legal language in the documents, which for non-legal trained personnel tends to obscure, rather than clarify meaning.

- The tenor of the will seemed clear when two prominent businessmen were named to be the 'trustees of **my** will and guardians of **my** children' and that '**my** trustees shall permit **my** wife Hannah Graham to carry on **my** business as inn keeper in South Brisbane'. (The bolding of **my** in the above point is not in the actual will. It seemed that the wording was somewhat indicative of male dominance at the time.)

- The will contains a considerable focus on the implementation and administration of a trust which was to be administered by the trustees.

- Graham clearly had a strong emotional link to his first daughter Ann, whose mother Catherine died when she was aged four. Early in the will, Nicol Stenhouse, the solicitor, recorded the only bequest to one of Graham's children:

  > I bequeath my silver watch and appendages to my daughter Ann.

- The will also specified that each of the trustees should be given £5 for the work they would do. The only real estate mentioned in the will was 'the house and tenement' in South Brisbane. These were the properties owned in Grey and Stanley Streets.

## Trustees

The trustees for the will were Richard James Coley of Brisbane and Benjamin Glennie of Brisbane. Coley lived in George Street and became the first Sergeant-at-Arms in the Queensland Parliament. At various times he was a sea captain, a merchant and a director on boards. Benjamin Glennie became a legend as a Church of England minister on the Darling Downs.

The reference to the trustees being made guardians of the children seems to be taking Hannah's authority as the mother away.

## Affidavits

A series of affidavits were made, and I have selected those that seemed to have an obvious implication on the final legal decision.

**21 January 1849:** Richard Cooley and Benjamin Glennie renounced their appointment as executors for Andrew Graham's will and had proctors appointed to replace them. These proctors were from the well-known Sydney legal firm of Holden and McCarthy. (George Kenyou Holden and William George McCarthy)

**2 February 1849:** Robert Little, solicitor, was to act as proctor for Hannah Graham and intended to apply to the Supreme Court for Letters of Administration regarding the goods, chattels and credits of Andrew Graham.

**9 March 1849:** Robert Banbury, clerk of Holden and McCarthy, searched the appropriate places at the Supreme Court, but no caveat had been entered at the Court. A caveat could be a special condition or limitation placed on the will.

**13 March 1849:** Hannah Graham requested an evaluation of the goods, chattel and credits of Andrew Graham. The persons recommended for this evaluation task were William Fitzpatrick, the Head Constable of Brisbane, and William Sheehan, who had been the innkeeper at *St Patrick's Tavern* from 1846 to 1848. In 1849 when the materials from old government buildings were sold, Sheehan purchased the material from what was known as the 'Old Barn'. Sheehan actually owned the block next to Andrew Graham's block in Stanley Street, so he obviously knew Hannah and Andrew Graham. *Ham's Map of Brisbane* shows that Fitzpatrick also owned eight allotments further down the Brisbane River from South Brisbane.

**13 March 1849**: Hannah Graham swore an oath before J C Wickham that the will being considered was the final will and testament of Andrew Graham.

**29 March 1849**: Hannah Graham was given the administrative rights to the goods, chattels and credits of Andrew Graham.

## Assessing Assets

William Fitzpatrick and William Sheehan were approved to assess the assets of Andrew Graham. These men may have completed this task, but the final document was prepared by Robert Little, a significant legal force in Brisbane.

Graham's assets focussed on the *Harp of Erin* inn in South Brisbane but were divided into two groups. One group related to the goods and chattels in the various rooms of the inn. These goods and chattels at the Harp of Erin inn have been outlined and discussed previously. The other group of potential assets were the debts associated with putting drinks 'on the tick' at the bar—allowing a member of the public to drink with the belief that they will pay later.

These records are from 1843 to 1848. Each record is dated, but they are not in a yearly sequence. The 'debts' are numbered, but for some reason the numbering commences at 44. The last number is 353. Various numbers are missing from the sequence and it is assumed that these people paid up at a previous date. In some instances, the names attributed to specific debts are not very helpful when endeavouring to assess their willingness to pay. The following four are listed as owing money to the inn: Fletcher bullock driver, Woodford, McCarthy at McKenzie and Mat of Golden Fleece.

The assessors went through the list and made short cryptic comments as to the potential for recovery of each debt. For example, there were a total of 115 assessments where the rating was either 'no good', 'do not know the man' or 'doubtful'. The assessment described as 'no good' was most likely used when it was thought there was no chance of a payment being made. A further 22 debts were associated with assessments of 'dead', 'left the district or country' or 'transported'.

There were very few positive assessments. One debt was apparently 'settled' and another was described as 'good'. Four debts contained a comment about 'contra and pay deductions'. In simple terms, the 'bad debts' of the inn represented a substantial amount of money. The process used to assess the bar debts of *Harp of Erin* probably did not equate with the current process described as forensic accounting, but it suited the state of development existing at the time in the rough and ready colony.

The list of the apparently unpaid bar debts extends for seven pages, and when totalled comes to £392/11/04. These debts extend over a period of six years, and assuming the accuracy of the data, reflects an enormous financial disaster for the *Harp of Erin* inn, and by implication to Hannah and her young family.

There was a substantial range in the value of individual bar debts. The largest and smallest individual bar debt on each of the seven pages and the assessor's comments are presented below.

## LARGE BAR DEBTS

| | | |
|---|---|---|
| Page 1 | Bill Cook—died three years ago. | £7/14/- |
| Page 2 | Captain Moffatt—no good dead. | £10/10/- |
| Page 3 | John McIntyre, Ipswich—disputed. | £8/9/6 |
| Page 4 | Jack Mayall—not known here. | £8/16/3 |
| Page 5 | Jack Slack—contra a/c supported. | £19/8/- |
| Page 6 | G S Tuckey—good. | £21/3/1 |
| Page 7 | Norman Charles —settled by contra a/c | £5/12/10 |

## SMALL BAR DEBTS

| | | |
|---|---|---|
| Page 1 | Dan Bryant—no good. | 2/- |
| Page 2 | Arthur Binstree—no good. | 4/- |
| Page 3 | Woodford—left district. | 2/9 |
| Page 4 | Jim Shea—no good. | 9/- |
| Page 5 | Billy Grey—no good. | 3/- |
| Page 6 | Jack Price—doubtful. | 5/- |
| Page 7 | George Mercatta —gone to California. | 4/4 |

The last three numbered debts are of considerable interest as a result of the named persons, the amount involved and the cryptic assessment. These are almost certainly not bar debts. In fact, the George Croft debt has been discussed earlier in this book, and it was an accommodation debt at the *Harp of Erin* inn.

14/06/1847   #349   Sutton W S     £21/-/1    No Good

31/05/1847   #353   Croft George   £26/18/3   No Good

No Date      #354   Ross Neil      £21/-/-    No Good

W S Sutton gave his work place as Kangaroo Point and advertised in the *Moreton Bay Courier* that he had pine and hardwood for sale. He was elected to the first municipal council for Brisbane, and in 1848 held the licence for the *Bush Commercial Hotel* where the brutal murder of Richard Cox occurred. This was the notorious case which cast suspicion on Patrick Mayne. Sutton was a well-known citizen, and it is difficult to understand why the apparent debt was not paid.

As reported elsewhere in this text, the Croft debt was genuine. George Croft was the man who established an amphitheatre in South Brisbane. There was disquiet about the wording in a song and the resultant criticism led to the theatre being closed. Croft, who was living at Graham's *Harp of Erin* inn, and the money owing represented unpaid accommodation costs.

There is no date provided for the Neil Ross entry. He had worked on Goomburra Station for some years. Neil and Isabella Ross lived in a house quite close to the Allora Crossing, and they eventually managed runs of their own. In 1844 Christopher Rolleston, the Crown Land Commissioner, described the Ross holding as small, being 20 square miles. By 1847 the *Moreton Bay Courier* reported that Ross had exported 36 bales of wool and some tallow in May and July of that year. Grace, the daughter of Neil and Isabella Ross, married Fred Bracker, an immensely successful pastoralist. These two families developed a strong relationship, and both Neil and Isabella Ross were buried on the Bracker property, Waroo, Macintyre Brook. It seems unlikely that with the resources available, the *Harp of Erin* debt was probably not that of Neil Ross from the Darling Downs. There may have been another Neil Ross in the Brisbane environs, or a person of this name may have passed through Brisbane. Another possibility was the accounting system in place at the inn did not work that well.

Given that the above three apparent 'debts' represented considerable purchasing power—enough for the annual salaries of two or more labourers—this was another serious blow to the assessment of Graham's assets.

## Hannah Takes Over

Soon after Graham's death in 1848, Hannah took over the liquor licence for the *Harp of Erin,* and the hotel's name was eventually changed to the *Steam Packet Hotel.* The precise date of the change in name of the hotel is unclear. Hannah may have changed the name of the inn to demonstrate her independence from past events and from a name given to the inn by Andrew.

By 1849 Hannah Graham was running an inn and looking after a family. In December of 1849 a 'to let' advertisement appeared in the *Moreton Bay Courier* under the name of Mrs Graham. This advertisement read as follows, and it was noted that Hannah was available 'Directly Opposite':

> COMFORTBLE FAMILY HOUSE, in Grey Street, South Brisbane, containing eleven rooms, with detached kitchen, out-houses etc. To a careful and permanent tenant, a reduced rent would be charged.
>
> Apply to Mrs Graham (Directly Opposite)

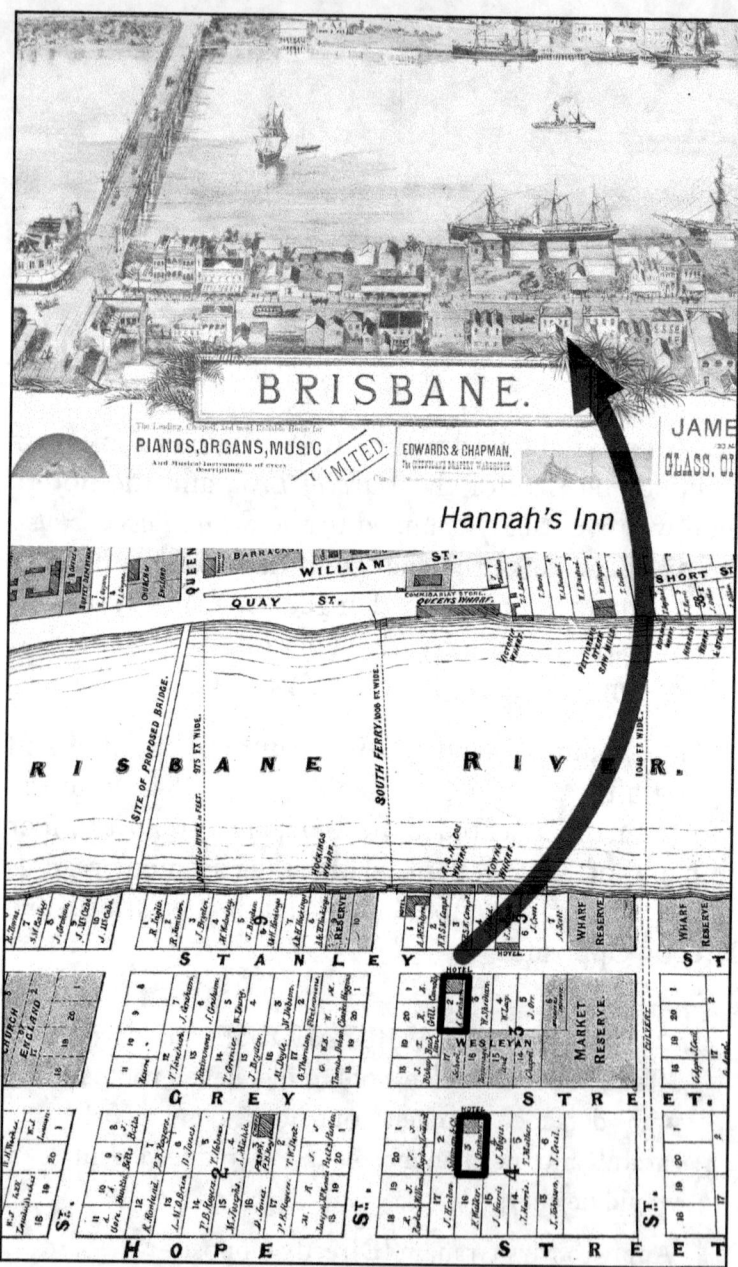

6. Hannah's inn on Stanley Street identified on map of Brisbane 1863 and lithograph of Brisbane 1888

This seems to suggest that Hannah intended to rent the initial building that had been the site of the *Harp of Erin* inn in Grey Street. She would continue to run an inn, but it was now in Stanley Street.

The December 1849 description of the *Harp of Erin*, Grey Street, in the *Moreton Bay Courier* mentions eleven rooms, detached kitchen and outhouses. When the wording of this advertisement is compared with the assessment of goods and chattels made in March 1849, there may appear to be some discrepancies, but these were probably deliberate in an attempt to attract tenants.

## Hannah and Frank Mercer

It is doubtful that Hannah's life in South Brisbane could ever be called simple. Hannah married Frank Mercer in June 1851. By November of that year, the *Moreton Bay Courier* reported that John McMahon pleaded guilty to the charge of stealing 'certain wearing apparel' belonging to Hannah and Frank Mercer.

When Hannah Graham married Frank Mercer, one of the witnesses was Miss Jessica Orr. Her father John, a butcher, had an allotment in South Brisbane very close to the *Harp of Erin*, Stanley Street site. In November 1854 the wedding of Jessica to John Wylie Wilson was announced in the *Moreton Bay Courier*. The Wilsons moved to Bowen and lived at Wylie Park. When Jessica died in 1897, John, her husband, became extremely depressed and committed suicide six months later.

It seemed that Hannah Graham may have been in Sydney in August 1847 and that she had clothing stolen. The *Sentinel* reported that wearing apparel belonging to Hannah Graham had been stolen, and the Quarter Sessions Court sentenced Elizabeth Cloud to three

## Hannah & Friends: Life in South Brisbane

months in prison with solitary confinement. This was in fact, not the Hannah Graham from South Brisbane, but it does reflect the harshness of punishment in the colony the Grahams lived in. Taking this a little further, it was noted that the case directly before that of Elizabeth Cloud involved a John Harrington who, having been convicted of stealing a roll of cloth, was sentenced to two years hard labour in irons.

Hannah's second husband, Frank Dawson Mercer, was born in Southwark, Surrey, in 1830 and was the son of Reverend Thomas Warren Mercer. Searches revealed the Reverend Mercer and his wife Sarah enrolled Frank and his elder brother at Merchant Taylor's School in London. This school was founded in 1561. It has always been considered an elite school with outstanding results.

Frank arrived in Moreton Bay aboard the *Fortitude* in 1849. This was the first of three ships organised by Dunmore Lang to bring the right type of citizens (Presbyterians) to grow cotton in 'Cooksland'. The first problem encountered by the *Fortitude* was it had to be quarantined on Moreton Island as a few cases of 'some infectious disease' had occurred during the voyage. The staunch spirit of the most devout Presbyterians, often with a Scottish background, would have been tested by a few days camping in tents on Moreton Island with a shortage of food. Worse was to come when they did land in Brisbane. They were told the promised blocks of land did not exist. Many of the arrivals were virtually dumped in what became known as Fortitude Valley. Given the extraordinary and disappointing arrival, it would not have been a surprise if these devout Presbyterian passengers formed gangs of marauding bushrangers.

Mercer was listed as being a 17-year-old 'agriculturalist' in the passenger records of the *Fortitude*. Unfortunately, this passenger list has been described as 'a mess on pieces of paper'. If Frank was born in 1830 and arrived in Brisbane in 1849, then he was 19 years old on arrival in the colony.

When newspapers are used as the major source of information regarding occurrences from many years ago, questions of validity and impartiality may be raised. In August 1909 the *Beaudesert Times* reported a segment from an article entitled *Birth of Free Brisbane* taken from the Brisbane Sun. This paragraph talks about Frank Dawson Mercer being the only innkeeper at Kangaroo Point. It also states that Mercer owned a racehorse called Major and that he was a good boxer and rider. *The Queenslander* published in August 1909 reported that the *Steam Packet Hotel* was run by Mrs Graham who 'married an old time sportsman Frank Mercer'. Unfortunately, verification checks of such comments can be extremely difficult, and what the paper reports, irrespective of accuracy, may in time become the truth.

No evidence was located confirming Mercer as a boxer. Frank was interested and involved in racing. There was evidence of a reasonably successful racehorse named Major, but it is uncertain if Frank ever owned this horse. In May 1856 the *Moreton Bay Courier* confirmed Frank as being at the Annual Brisbane Races held on a recently constructed course at New Farm. These races were conducted over three days, with the first day, Tuesday, being declared a holiday. Frank was associated with two horses, Verbena and Catch-me-if-you-can.

When Nehemiah Bartley's book *Opals and Agates* was published in 1892, it contained specific information regarding Mercer. In summary, he described Mercer as having the only hotel on 'the Point' (Kangaroo Point) and suggested that Mercer was 'fast'. In such a connotation, this old-fashioned word of disapproval could even mean a concern about a person's moral principles.

Bartley believed that the horse Major was owned by Mercer and reported that close to Mercer's death, his horse Veno won the £1000 challenge race between NSW and Victoria. The *Moreton Bay Courier* 1857-58 reports the various challenge races involving Veno, but persons other than Mercer were listed as the owner of the horse.

From Mercer's arrival in Moreton Bay in 1849 to 1852, very little information is available regarding his activities. There was considerable awareness regarding the potential value of discovering gold in a particular district. In 1851 Mercer was among a group of Moreton Bay residents contributing to a financial reward for the person who first discovered gold in the Moreton Bay District. Frank was willing to contribute £10 toward this fund, but no evidence was located of the reward being collected.

In September 1852 Henry Buckley was Chair of a committee set up to prepare a petition requesting the separation of Queensland from NSW. Buckley, who hailed from Yorkshire, spent some time in Sydney and arrived in Moreton Bay in 1849. He was involved in many businesses, including being the agent for the Australasian Steam Navigation Company. He later became a magistrate and a member of parliament. As chair of the separation petition, he appointed Mercer as the collector of funds for South of the Brisbane River. It is unclear what knowledge and links Frank Mercer had south of the river. Two years later, in 1853, Mercer placed an advertisement in the *Moreton Bay Courier* indicating that persons interested in letting the *Logan Hotel* should contact him at the *Queens Arms Hotel*, Kangaroo Point. The immediate reaction was to query where the Logan Hotel was, presumably south of the Brisbane River. It was actually in Grey Street, South Brisbane, a fact verified by correspondence from the *Logan River Family History Society Inc*, 28/03/2020. Henry Twiss held the licence of the *Logan* from 1850 to 1851 and, as a business competitor, would have been known to Hannah.

Data in the NSW Archives provides evidence that Mercer took up the licence for the *Queens Arms Hotel* at Kangaroo Point on 6 December 1853. In early 1854 advertisements in the *Moreton Bay Courier* extolled the stables, paddocks, food, alcohol and hospitality at the *Queens Arms*. Mercer appeared to be taking his responsibilities at the *Queens Arms* seriously, as in 1854 he advertised for an experienced cook and waiter, indicating that references were required. By September 1854 William Wilson had taken over the licence for the *Queens Arms* until 1856.

Mercer held the licence for the *Queens Arms* at Kangaroo Point for less than 12 months. Hannah Mercer worked at the inn where Frank held the licence, and it is worth noting that newspapers often referred to the establishment as being Hannah Mercer's.

In early 1854 the *Moreton Bay Courier* reported in several issues of the paper, details regarding the brutal bashing and eventual death of Stephen Swords. This incident took place in a hut not far from Mercer's *Queens Arms*, Kangaroo Point. An ex-convict, John Hanley, was charged with the murder. Hannah Mercer was called to give evidence as she had served Hanley and others on the Saturday preceding the bashing. She also served Hanley and Swords on the Sunday. Hanley received the death sentence, but this was somehow avoided, and Hanley served 5 years hard labour. In July 1854 the *Moreton Bay Courier* was outraged at this decision and reported the following:

> Few of our readers can fail to be startled by the announcement that John Hanley ... Has been saved from death. ... is to undergo a punishment usually awarded in petty cases of dishonesty—five year's hard labour.

This case involving the murder of Swords had implications for a decision later made by Wickham. On 4 February 1854 the *Moreton Bay Courier* reported that F D Mercer was 'guilty to an information' for allowing alcohol to be sold on a Sunday and was fined 40/- with costs of 5/6. I assume that 'guilty to an information' was an unusual charge and seems to mean that information from a reputable source has contacted the magistrates regarding the licensee selling alcohol on Sunday.

In the 1850s Reverend Henry Stobart was the tutor for two young English Lords during their tour of colonial NSW. Stobart was asked by Frank Mercer's father (Reverend Thomas Mercer) to visit his son Frank. Mercer had arrived on the *Fortitude* described as an 'agriculturalist'. The *Truth,* in October 1915, claimed he had left England as he was in substantial debt. The meeting between Stobart and the innkeeper Mercer was presented in the following manner:

> The chaplain-tutor said your father told me that you were a landowner and sheep breeder. Mercer responded, well you would not have had me do anything so unkind as to tell the truth to the old man. (p.11)

Mercer, like Hannah's previous husband Andrew Graham, entered the hotel business and in December 1853 held the licence for the *Queens Arms Hotel*, Kangaroo Point. Given his recent arrival, it is seems possible that Hannah may have assisted in the purchase of stock and furniture for the *Queens Arms*. In 1851 the *NSW Government Gazette* reported that Hannah Graham had purchased a 33¼ perch allotment. This purchase was described as being Section 12, Allotment 22 in Adelaide Street, North Brisbane. It seems that this was the only land purchase made by Hannah in North Brisbane. The cost of Hannah's purchase was £41/11/3. It is noted that other well-known citizens such as Tom Douse, Darby McGrath and William Thornton purchased allotments in Section 12. At this time of her life, she probably had the resources to assist Mercer to become the licensee of an inn. There are other possibilities; Mercer may have worked and acquired money.

The various early colonial newspapers contained articles about gaining access to quality workers. In 1853 Frank Mercer found that it was difficult to both obtain and retain good servants. He charged Thomas Friend with absenting himself from his formal hired service. Mercer was completely dissatisfied with Friend's previous work and did not want to re-employ him. The punishment received by Friend was 14 days in the Brisbane goal.

Mercer reapplied for the *Queens Arms* licence in April 1854, but his application was rejected by Wickham, William A Duncan and John Ferriter. The number of magistrates on the bench may have been small, but they were significant members of the Moreton Bay District. Wickham had been the first officer and then Captain of the *Beagle* with Charles Darwin aboard. Upon retirement, he initially became the police magistrate for Moreton Bay. Duncan had obtained a classical education and then schooled himself in foreign languages. He was an ardent supporter of Catholicism and was involved in several publishing ventures. Later, Duncan was appointed sub-controller of customs and then as a member of the important National Education Board. John Ferriter was a successful squatter holding such runs as Wivenhoe and Barambah. He was also a JP at Ipswich.

Initially, the reason for this rejection of the licence appeared to stem from a breach of the Licensed Victuallers Act by Mercer when he served members of the *Eagles* crew between the hours of 10.00 and 11.00pm. Evidence regarding this breach was provided by Constables Booth and Walker. In addition to the charge of serving alcohol outside approved hours, the same constables reported that Mercer did not have his inn keeper's light burning all night. He was fined an additional 5/- with costs of 8/6 for this breach.

Fate has a strange way of intruding into reality. The case regarding the breach of the act by Mercer reported in the *Moreton Bay Courier* was followed by a case involving John McCabe from the *Commercial Hotel*. McCabe had also served customers outside the approved hours. McCabe's *Commercial Hotel* was a short distance from Mercer's but on the other side of Stanley Street. The customers at the *Commercial* were those stalwarts and enforcers of the legal system in Brisbane, Constables Booth and Walker.

## Frank Mercer v's Arthur Lyon

In October 1853 an unusual case was conducted in the Water Police Court, Brisbane. This case was between Frank Mercer and Arthur Sydney Lyon. Lyon had arrived in Moreton Bay from Sydney and although the population was just over 2000, he expressed a desire to commence a newspaper. The first edition of the *Moreton Bay Courier* appeared in 1846. Over the next several years, Lyon was responsible for the introduction of the first four Moreton Bay newspapers and is considered a pioneer in the development of Queensland newspapers.

For a period of time, Lyon lived at Frank and Hannah's inn, and during the court case the possibility was raised that he owed the Mercers money for accommodation. Lyon's health had not been good, and he had had several 'paralytic attacks'. It sounded as if Lyon may have been depressed as he believed that a change in location and occupation might help. He moved to Stradbroke Island and became a fisherman. Lyon initiated the court case saying Mercer and others came out to Stradbroke Island and took his boat. Clarity was not obvious in this case and there was an implication that Mercer and two others pooled money so that a fishing boat could be purchased for Lyon. It was suggested that 'the fisherman' might deliver some fish to Mercer. This did not happen. Perhaps there was also an expectation that money for the boat was to be repaid. The case against Mercer was dismissed.

As Lyon lived in Mercer's inn for some time, Hannah obviously knew him quite well. We do not know how she felt about this case. Perhaps the case was considered 'men's business' and Hannah just continued to do her jobs.

## Bush Inn and the Mercers

Frank Mercer, having failed to gain a liquor licence in the Brisbane district, applied for a licence in September 1854 from the Ipswich Bench. This application was for 'the house at Cunningham's Gap' which was actually Archibald Young's old *Bush Inn* on the Fassifern. It is highly likely that Mercer knew that the Ipswich Bench had received a letter from Wickham. On 16 September 1854 The *Moreton Bay Courier* reported this letter in the following manner:

> (That this) applicant was unfit to hold a Publican's Licence, he having sold grog on a Sunday to a person at Kangaroo Point who was subsequently murdered.

The application was held over for 2 months and then in December 1854 the Ipswich Bench awarded the Cunninghams Gap licence to F D Mercer.

Colonel Charles Gray, Mr Henry Mort and Mr Richard Smith were the magistrates who approved Mercer's application. Apparently, these magistrates were not greatly concerned with Mercer's breach of the Victualler's Act in Brisbane nor with Wickham's annoyance relating to the serving of alcohol at Frank Mercer's on a Sunday and the link to Sword's murder.

The records of the NSW Archives show that Mercer actually gained the *Bush Inn* licence twice in 1854, on 17 April and 5 December. The magistrates who supported Mercer's application were three rather noted colonial persons. Gray was a highly distinguished British soldier who in 1853 was appointed police magistrate in Ipswich. In 1848 Mort took up land to the west of Grandchester where a now heritage-listed site known as Franklyn Vale Station was established. Smith established a boiling down works in 1849 at an 83 acre site known as Town Marie on the Bremer River. Despite insolvency, he became a member of parliament and eventually a land commissioner.

The gaining of a licence for the *Bush Inn* did not solve the problems experienced by the Mercers. In February 1855 their daughter Sarah Campbell Mercer died at age four (born 4 April 1851—died 8 February 1855). Sarah drowned in a nearby creek. Some years later, the *Queensland Times* presented an entirely different cause of death for Sarah Mercer. On 7 January 1938 the newspaper incorrectly explained the death of Sarah Mercer:

> Sarah age four fell a victim to diphtheria or inflammatory croup, as it was then called. The child was buried beside Warrill Creek.

There are three memorials commemorating deaths in the Fassifern Memorial Cemetery. One of these is for

Sarah Campbell Mercer (1855), and the other two are Alexander Balbi (1867) and Anders Nielsen (1887).

Sarah's death in 1855 added to the sorrow Hannah experienced with the death of previous children.

On 21 August 1852 the *Moreton Bay Courier* reported that Lousia Ann Mercer died aged ten weeks. On 11 June 1853 the same newspaper printed a death notice for Lousia Anna Mercer aged 8 days. Both these deaths took place while Sarah Campbell Mercer was in what might be described as her 'toddler' years. Unfortunately, repeated infantile mortality was experienced by many families during the mid-1800s. It is difficult to reflect on the life of Hannah and not feel a rush of compassion for her.

While Frank and Hannah were living at the *Bush Inn* in 1857, George Pratten, the surveyor, drew up a possible plan for a township named Fassifern. There was a need for townships in the developing Darling Downs, but other sites were given a higher priority. This plan did not turn into a reality, but Pratten had named a street where the *Bush Inn* was originally located as Mercer's Place.

## Frank Mercer and Champoo

Frank Mercer was witness to a dispute reported in the *Moreton Bay Courier* on 21 February 1857 between John Orr and a man of Chinese origin called Champoo. This name was probably one of convenience as in later newspaper issues the names of Shampoo, Kim and Kimpoo were also used. The newspaper referred to Champoo as a celestial, which the *Cambridge Dictionary* defines 'as or from the sky or outside this world.' It was reported that this celestial spoke and understood very little English. To ensure that justice appeared to be done, Champoo was granted an interpreter. The newspaper assessed the interpreter's skills in English as rather similar to those of Champoo. The interpreter and Champoo were sworn in using a process probably viewed as unusual in the colonial courts. A saucer was broken on the floor. This was taken as a sign that if they did not tell the truth their souls would be similarly destroyed.

The incident took place when Frank Mercer and John Orr sought protection from rain at a house apparently owned by Orr, but one in which Champoo lived. An argument ensued and involved some physical contact.

Orr contended that Champoo chased him with a knife, and Mercer supported this statement. The decision was that Champoo was to be bound over by various financial sureties to ensure he would keep the peace for three months. This is like what is now called a good behaviour bond.

Champoo unfortunately did not attend to all the financial requirements and was sent to goal in Brisbane for three months. The life of this unfortunate Chinese man continued on a downhill trajectory. In March 1858 he was charged with stabbing Alfred Owen, the superintendent at Yandilla Station. He was found guilty and sentenced to two years hard labour on the roads. In 1860 he was charged with murdering Garrick Burns, a shepherd at Clifton Station. A jury of 12 found Champoo guilty but added a strong recommendation for mercy. Justice Alfred Lutwyche ruled that Champoo should be hanged for murdering Burns. On 25 September 1860 the *Maitland Mercury* reported that the verdict was amended to life in prison with the first three years in irons. At an unknown date, Champoo was moved into Woogaroo Asylum.

Frank Mercer's observation of an incident involving Champoo provided an opportunity to have a quick glance at some interesting aspects of the legal system that Hannah and friends were operating in during the 1850s. Fisher (2012), in a consideration of 'ethnic presence' in early Brisbane, noted that a number of Chinese had congregated in South Brisbane as compared to North Brisbane.

## Frank Mercer and Horses

Throughout the 1840s and 1850s the colonial newspapers of NSW contained numerous advertisements relating to the theft or disappearance of horses. This is probably no surprise as in the Moreton Bay and Darling Downs districts the population was sparse and scattered. There were few constables or fences and a great deal of bush and scrub. A considerable proportion of the population had obtained free passage to NSW as the result of a legal decision. The rehabilitation acquired in the penal colonies was such that in a number of instances it enhanced rather than minimised an exile's desire and capacity to jump on a horse and gallop off. Horse theft was not restricted to exiles. In 1858 Archibald Young, for example, the successful licensee of the Samford Run, was charged with illegally riding a horse belonging to the highly influential Patrick Mayne. Actually, the horse was used in a stock round up on the Samford Run.

Mercer placed an advertisement in the *Moreton Bay Courier* in 1852 offering a £1 reward for information regarding a bay filly that had disappeared from South Brisbane. In 1852 an Aborigine named Jacky was charged by Mercer with taking one of his horses and riding after cattle. The punishment was a warning about using other people's property. Another advertisement appeared in 1855 offering a £5 reward for information regarding the whereabouts of a valuable bay horse. Information relating to this horse could be given to F D Mercer, *Bush Inn*, Cunninghams Gap, R E Dix, Brisbane or Marcus Berkman, Warwick. Dix and Berkman were well known identities in the region, suggesting Mercer may have had a network of contacts in the 1850s.

# Frank: Insolvency and Death

In March 1856 the *Moreton Bay Courier* and the *North Australian, Ipswich and General Advertiser* carried a notice from F D Mercer requesting that his creditors contact him as soon as possible with details of their claims. Clearly Mercer was aware of his unsatisfactory financial position and this came to a head in 1857.

The *Moreton Bay Courier* reported a sad note concerning the Mercers in May 1857. An order by Judge Samuel Milford stated that F D Mercer was insolvent with a deficit of £821/6/1. Mercer explained that his insolvency arose from four causes.

1. He had an application refused for the *Queens Arms Hotel*, but a large amount of stock was purchased before the decision was made.

2. The purchase of the *Bush Inn*, Cunninghams Gap cost £784 and further expenditure was involved relocating his family to the *Bush Inn*.

3. He had experienced an ongoing illness.

4. He had been unemployed for the past 18 months and thus could not commence paying off his debts.

Just five months later, Mercer applied for a certificate of discharge from insolvency, but it is not obvious where the money came from. Later in this book, it is mentioned that Hannah owed money to Nehemiah Bartley. Perhaps this debt originated with Hannah borrowing from Bartley to settle Frank's insolvency debt.

Warning signs were evident as early as April 1855 when Thomas Alford informed the *Moreton Bay Courier* that Mercer would like to sell the *Bush Inn* by private agreement, and if this did not work, a public auction may be implemented. This was after the death of their four-year-old daughter and a growing debt problem.

Mercer died in October 1857, and this must have been a difficult time for Hannah. Perhaps she knew her husband's illness was critical and that she needed to step forward even more than usual as the financial provider for her family. On the death of Andrew Graham in 1848, Hannah had previously been required to sort out the mess that arose from a will and numerous small debts owed to the inn.

Mercer did leave a will that was made before he left the United Kingdom for NSW. Administration of his effects was granted to the Rev Thomas Warren Mercer of North Allerton in the County of Yorkshire. These effects were valued at under £300.

## Hannah and Genteel Board

For some years there had been a *Caledonian Hotel* in North Brisbane. In late 1856 and into 1857, Hannah either owned or leased a site known as the *Caledonian Hotel*. It initially appeared that Hannah had moved some of her business interests to north of the river. This was incorrect, as the records of the *NSW Archives* show that in 1853-1854 William Melville held the licence for the *Caledonian Hotel* in Grey Street, South Brisbane. Various advertisements appeared between October 1856 and April 1857 in the *North Australian, Ipswich and General Advertiser* stating the premises were available for rent and that Hannah could be contacted on site. Single and family rooms were available. Hannah stated that she would welcome her friends, inhabitants from the Northern Districts and visitors to Brisbane. Meals were provided; there was good stabling and well-watered paddocks. On 28 October 1856 Hannah Mercer advertised this accommodation under the rather interesting heading of 'Genteel Board and Lodging House'. Given the definition of genteel, it would seem that Hannah was hoping to attract well-mannered and respectable clients. It could well be that she wanted 'boarders' from a social group with the capacity to pay their accounts. Precisely how long the renting activity at the *Caledonian* continued for is unknown. Hannah applied for a liquor licence on the 20 April 1859 and was given a period of time to carry out some improvements and repairs. However, by May 1859 Hannah was running the *Royal Oak Hotel* in Grey Street, South Brisbane.

The two allotments purchased by Andrew Graham in South Brisbane were utilised as inns at various times. Different names were used for these hotels—the *Harp of Erin* and the *Steam Packet* being the most frequently adopted. It is unclear why the names were changed, but it is assumed that Hannah perceived the changes were in some way linked to business advantage. Relating the story of Hannah and her friends is increased in complexity due to the name changes of the business sites.

On 5 March 1859 the *Moreton Bay Courier* carried an advertisement for the renting of the *Steam Packet Hotel*. The site was described as being an excellent central location and one where an extensive business could be organised. Applicants interested in applying were advised to contact Mrs Mercer at the *Royal Oak*, South Brisbane or William Sheehan, North Brisbane. Sheehan was a long-time associate of Hannah and Andrew Graham.

The *Moreton Bay Courier* reported that in August 1859 John Melville had commenced a 'private boarding establishment' at the site of the old *Steam Packet Hotel*. Later in August, Melville placed a more detailed advertisement in the *Moreton Bay Courier*:

Brian Hansford

## MELVILLE'S PRIVATE BOARDING ESTABLISHMENT
(Late Steam Packet Hotel)
Opposite the ASN Company Wharf, South Brisbane
NB - Good stables and well-watered paddocks

Perhaps this boarding establishment did not achieve the financial returns hoped for as a month later, in September 1859, Melville reopened the *Steam Packet Hotel*.

The Melville family arrived on the first and most contentious of the Dunmore Lang chartered ships, the *Fortitude*, in 1849. Two of their sons were named John and William, and it seems likely that these were the Melvilles involved in dealings with Hannah in the 1850s.

The major reason inns existed was for the sale of alcohol, and it is probably no surprise that Hannah experienced an ongoing range of irritating occurrences. Inn closing time was officially 10.00pm, but one hot and humid January night in 1858, she left the door open until 11.00pm. Although no customers came into the *Royal Oak*, she was fined 5/-. Hannah's argument she did not own a clock probably did not help. On a night in 1859, a fight occurred at the *Royal Oak*. Reports in the *Moreton Bay Courier* during the 1840s and 50s suggest fights were rather frequent events. The fight at the *Royal Oak* in 1859 involved William Baxter, who charged Thomas Denham with malicious wounding. The verdict was not guilty. Hannah's son, John Graham, was serving in the hotel that night and was called as a witness.

## Hannah & Friends: Life in South Brisbane

A Thomas Denham had been noted as being in difficulties with the law by the *Moreton Bay Courier* in March and May 1850. In *R v Denham* (1850) NSWSupCMB 11 it is reported that Denham was convicted of larceny and sentenced to three months hard labour in Brisbane goal. Comments in the *Moreton Bay Courier* and the Supreme Court documents suggested Denham was 'feeble minded' and 'very confused'. The judge, Roger Therry, suggested that hard labour should be adjusted in accordance with Denham's mental capacities and that after he had served the sentence, some protection should be organised for the man. Was this protection arranged? Was this the same Thomas Denham who turned up at the *Royal Oak* in 1859?

One evening in 1859 at the *Royal Oak*, Hannah allowed music to be played, and she was warned that this was strictly illegal. Hannah was informed that in future she must apply for a licence for such entertainment.

On 5 March 1859 Hannah was again called to provide evidence in a court case. It was alleged that James Burns had assaulted and robbed Peter Schick on the Ipswich Road. Burns denied the charge. Hannah's evidence stated that on the day before the alleged crime she had seen Burns with Schick. Burns was charged with highway robbery and attempted murder; he had viciously beaten Schick with a stick. The jury found Burns guilty of the crime but recommended mercy. Judge Alfred Lutwyche ruled that as the crime was premeditated, cruel and vicious, death was the appropriate sentence. In July 1859 the penalty was commuted to 15 years hard labour with the first three in irons.

## Hannah and 1860 Court Cases

During 1860 the *Moreton Bay Courier* and other papers in the area reported on related cases that occurred in the Police Court, Brisbane, June 1860 and the Supreme Court, Brisbane, August 1860. These cases involved the apparent theft of a horse. The participants in the court cases were the initial owner of the horse, James Fitzgerald, a freeholder from the Logan River. Fitzgerald had been in the Logan area since 1842 and purchased 900 acres there. Fitzgerald said he had rented the horse to Jeremiah (Jerry) Harney. Hannah Mercer explained that she had purchased the horse while Harney was a paying guest at her inn in South Brisbane.

In the Police Court, Hannah reported that Harney had taken up accommodation at her inn for 4 weeks. Witnesses who had called at the inn stated that Harney seemed to be drunk all the time. Hannah claimed she purchased the horse from Harney and that she had a document to verify this. There were two women who worked for Hannah, Sarah Greenwood and Annie Graham, who were involved in the preparation and signing of the document. Annie Graham was described as the stepdaughter of Hannah, and Sarah Greenwood was probably the daughter of the Greenwoods who leased a hotel in the Grey Street area. There was some concern relating to the writing on the document and comments about conflicting evidence. Charles Lilley, acting for Hannah, had considerable difficulties obtaining sensible answers from Harney. At one point he told Harney, 'this is not a joke' and later in the case described Harney as 'an individual with a head like a sugar loaf'. Lilley said the case had broken and should be withdrawn. This was done and the horse was returned to the owner, Fitzgerald.

The 1860 case in the Supreme Court focussed on a charge that Harney had stolen Fitzgerald's horse. This case covered similar ground to the Police Court case and again there was concern about the document. It was intended to show Hannah had purchased the horse and had a legal document supporting this claim. There were suggestions that the document may have been tampered with by persons unknown, and Harney again was a difficult witness. The case again collapsed and Harney was released.

Judge Alfred Lutwyche took an unusual stance on the completion of this case. He asked that Annie Graham reappear in court and addressed her in the following manner:

> It is 'my public duty to give you a public caution. Be careful when you enter the witness box not to swear to anything you know to be false. You may now go'.

It is obvious that Lutwyche was challenging the validity of the evidence given by Annie Graham.

There is an additional comment to be made regarding Jeremiah Harney. A search of newspapers revealed that six years previously, in 1854, Harney had been charged with stealing a horse from Mr Ramsay, South Brisbane. The presiding judge, Mr Justice John Dickinson, noted that drunkenness was involved in the case and that it was possible mental imbecility may have been evidenced in the courtroom. He dismissed the case.

The *Moreton Bay Courier* on 6 December 1860 contained a wanted notice from Hannah stating:

> Wanted, a person of considerable experience, for a situation of HOUSEKEEPER. She would not object to attending to the cooking in a small family, or to go to the country. Apply to Mrs Mercer's Hotel, South Brisbane.

Interpreting and probably extrapolating the above notice is complex. It is interesting that there is no mention of working at an inn. Suggesting that the 'housekeeper' would do the cooking for a small family and should be prepared to move out of the city may be a prediction of what occurs in mid-1861.

## Hannah Moves to Ipswich

The annual liquor licensing meeting for the Brisbane area was held in April 1861. Fifteen licences were granted and 10 were approved with conditions or were held over for a month. Perhaps one of the most interesting applications granted subject to a caution was that for T Chambers at the *Sawyer's Arms*, North Brisbane. The caution that Chambers had to meet was that he must 'not supply patients in the hospital with liquor.' Hannah Mercer applied for a new licence for a house at Kangaroo Point. This was rejected. Charles Lilley spoke in support of Hannah's application:

> Mrs Mercer was a very old publican, and had always conducted her house in an orderly manner.

The matter was then put to a vote, which resulted in seven voting against the application and four in favour. The application was rejected. No reasons were given for this outcome.

The rejection of the licence application in 1861 was almost certainly linked to the 1860 cases regarding Jeremiah Harney and the stolen horse. These cases seemed contentious, as newspaper reports appeared to suggest that witnesses may have provided inaccurate answers; one witness may have had mental problems and a document may have been tampered with. There is no doubt the cases were messy and became even murkier with the addition of alcoholism. Even if Hannah Mercer was an innocent victim in this legal quagmire, a number of magistrates decided to demonstrate their displeasure.

It is worth noting that when Hannah's husband Frank lost the support of the licensing magistrates in Brisbane, he moved out to the Fassifern; Hannah's decision was to move to Ipswich. She applied for the licence of the *Union Hotel,* and this was granted. This hotel was described by the Ipswich magistrates as being at or near One-Mile Creek or One-Mile Bridge. The 'one-mile' expression was used to demonstrate this location was about one mile from Ipswich where there was a bridge crossing the Bremer River. There is little doubt that moving from South Brisbane would have been difficult for Hannah.

## Hannah's Death

Hannah died at the *Union Hotel* on 30 November 1862. Charles Chubb, a prominent Ipswich lawyer who became Mayor of Ipswich in 1877, acting on behalf of a creditor, informed the Ipswich Police Court that a responsible person should be appointed to take charge of the One-Mile Creek premises until the Letters of Administration were taken out. James Mehan, a member of a family with considerable experience in the management of inns, undertook this task. By 10 December 1862 a Supreme Court notice appeared in the *Courier* making it clear that Hannah apparently owed Nehemiah Bartley money. This notice commenced with the following preamble:

> To the next of kin of Hannah Mercer, late of Ipswich, in the Colony of Queensland, Widow, licensed inn keeper, deceased. (And went on to ask why) ... the goods, chattels, and credits ... should not be committed to Nehemiah Bartley.

The *Australian Dictionary of Biography* described Bartley as a 'merchant', 'first commercial traveller in Queensland', 'collected orders on horseback', 'kept diaries', 'an author' and whose diaries seemed to suggest he 'had an obsessive interest in women'.

Despite Ipswich post office reporting an unclaimed letter addressed to 'the executors of the late Mrs H Mercer', no will or probate documents for Hannah were located. There is no doubt that Hannah died intestate.

The next of kin were invited to appear before the court on 4 January 1863. If they could not personally attend, they were advised to appoint a proctor, a legal practitioner, to appear. The next of kin or their proctors were invited to show sufficient cause why the assets of Hannah should 'not be committed to Nehemiah Bartley'. The notice concluded with a comment that Daniel Foley Roberts, an experienced Brisbane solicitor, had been appointed the proctor for Bartley.

Hannah was buried at Ipswich General Cemetery, and although burials commenced at this site in 1844, no records were officially kept until 1868.

A death certificate was obtained providing additional details regarding the life and death of Hannah. The registrar completing the certificate, William Herden, apparently wrote what he heard and assumed there was no need for a second 'h' in the word Hannah. William Herden was a prominent citizen in early Ipswich.

The death certificate record shows that Hannah was seen on the day of her death, 30 November, by Dr O'Doherty. The registrar appears to have had difficulty with the spelling of O'Doherty as an ink splatter partially covers an additional 'y' in the name. The doctor's report stated Hannah had died from dipsomania and that the episode had lasted four weeks. Dipsomania is an old word meaning something like a craving for alcohol.

7. Dr Kevin Izod O'Doherty signed
Hannah's death certificate 1862

Sadly, Hannah had become an alcoholic. The signature on Hannah's death certificate was that of Dr Kevin Izod O'Doherty, an Irishman transported to Tasmania for what was described as treason-felony. O'Doherty was politically active in Ireland and became a convict in 1848 largely for his role in publishing the *Irish Tribune*. Despite this conviction, as he was pardoned in 1854, O'Doherty later held positions in the Queensland and Irish parliaments. He has an entry in the *Australian Dictionary of Biography,* and in 1981 Dr Ross Patrick delivered the Memorial Clem Lack Oration, at Kelvin Grove, on 'From Convict to Doctor: The Life of Kevin O'Doherty'.

Hannah was buried the day after her death on 1 December 1862. The undertaker was George Drowden whose business was in Brisbane Street, Ipswich. Newspaper advertisements for Drowden's business stated he was a cabinetmaker, upholster and undertaker. Hannah did have relatives in Brisbane, but given the short lapse of time between death and burial, it would have been quite difficult for such persons to make the journey in time.

The certificate named Pierce Power 'Minister of the Church of Rome' as the celebrant at the burial service. Contact was made with John Rossiter, an excellent source of Ipswich historical information. I asked him about a priest named Pierce Power in Ipswich. He said this was not the name of a priest at that time, nor was there a priest with a similar name. He did note that there was a Catholic priest in Ipswich for an extremely short period ending in 1862. This priest apparently did not satisfy the hierarchy of the church and was quickly moved on. He was French and the correct name was Perecusse. It was fortunate that registrar Herden managed to get the first letter 'P' in the name correct.

It may have been anticipated that the names of relatives would be recorded as witnesses to the burial. This was not the case as two well-known Ipswich citizens were named, Christopher Gorry and Godfrey O'Rourke. Gorry (JP) was the Ipswich saddler and was deeply involved in the town's development. When Gorry died in March 1893, the *Queensland Times, Ipswich Herald and General Advertiser* were most eloquent in their comments and spoke of him as 'the Father of Ipswich'. O'Rourke was a successful Ipswich businessman who was involved in a number of activities. The *Courier* noted that in December 1862, he had completed 'water works' for Ipswich. He was probably best known for holding the licence of the *Cottage of Content Inn* for a number of years. With a name such as the *Cottage of Content*, extraordinary images are conjured up of an inn where happiness, peace and goodwill toward mankind existed. Given some knowledge of inns at that time, these images are grossly distorted and incorrect.

The original *Cottage of Content* still operates at Carey, Herefordshire (UK) on the Wye River and some parts of the structure date back to 1485.

It has to be remembered that Hannah had lived in this area previously. Her husband Frank lost the support of the Brisbane magistrates and failed to get his liquor licence renewed. In 1854 the Ipswich magistrates granted him the licence for the *Bush Inn*. Although this inn was described as being at Cunninghams Gap, it was actually on Warrill Creek in the area known as the Fassifern, a short day's horse ride from Ipswich. The Mercer's time at the *Bush Inn* was tragic as their four-year-old daughter Sarah died in a flood. This was the third child they had lost since 1852. Frank became ill and got into serious financial difficulties and was declared insolvent. He died in 1857. It is possible that the Mercers knew such people as Gorry and O'Rourke while trying to make a go of things at the *Bush Inn*.

William Herden, the registrar of deaths, was required to answer a specific question relating to Hannah's children. This question required the registrar to write down Hannah's children 'in order of birth, their names and ages.' Herden apparently could not do this, so what he provided was the number of children living and those who had died. He wrote that there were '3 boys living and 3 girls plus 1 boy dead.'

The three boys living were John Joshua Graham, Andrew Hamilton Graham and Frank Dawson Mercer. The three girls and one boy who had died were Lousia Anna Mercer who lived 8 days, Lousia Ann Mercer who lived 10 weeks, Sarah Campbell Mercer who lived four years and Richard Graham who had died at 11 years of age.

The accuracy of some early colonial death certificates has been queried, particularly those arising in remote and isolated settings. There is even the possibility that the people reporting the death did not know the dead person. The registrars did the best they could with the people who were available. In some instances, the dates provided and spelling of names were approximations.

## *Supreme Court and Hannah's Children*

Hannah died on 30 November 1862 and within a few days, a Supreme Court notice appeared indicating that Hannah owed Nehemiah Bartley a sum of money and he was seeking access to any assets previously owned by Hannah. It was suggested that there should be a legal settlement reached in early January 1863. Hannah was intestate, and this settlement appears not to have taken place. There were hearings of the Supreme Court on 1 and 2 April 1863. These hearings were before the Chief Justice, Sir James Cockle.

The *Courier* on 1 April, 1863 contained the following notice:

SUPREME COURT
In Equity
(Before his Honour the Chief Justice)

EX PARTE ANNIE GRAHAM, JOHN GRAHAM, AND ANDREW GRAHAM

This was a petition by the above mentioned infants praying the appointment of Henri Wilson Hassler as a receiver of the rents and profits of the real estate of their late father, Andrew Graham, and guardian of their persons.

The matter was ordered to stand over until the next day to allow the above-named infants to come into court.

The Latin term *ex parte* is used in the above notice and means 'for one party'. An *ex parte* order is a temporary order benefiting one party and in this order was intended to benefit the three named Graham children.

The reports in the *Courier* and *North Queenslander and Queensland Advertiser* confirm the following. The Supreme Court met the next day (2 April) with two of the three previously named children in attendance. Although the Chief Justice presided, it was the Queensland Attorney General, Radcliffe Pring, who addressed the court. Following introductory comments by Pring, his Honour directed:

> the appointment of Henri Wilson Hassler, chief clerk in the office for the Engineer for Roads as next friend of the above named infants, receiver of the rents and profits of the real estate of their deceased father, and guardian of the persons of two of the infants, Annie Graham and Andrew Graham, during their respective minorities.

It is rather complex to interpret what occurred in early April 1863. The second meeting of the Supreme Court named Annie and Andrew as the two recipients of the earnings of their father's real estate assets. John Graham, initially named as a recipient, had died and was thus deleted from the named recipients.

Andrew Graham died in 1848 and legal action directed that the money arising from Graham's real estate assets was to be controlled by Hannah until her death. The legal system apparently had a responsibility to see that this money now went to Andrew's children. H W Hassler accepted this task, but he also was named as guardian until the children reached adulthood at 21 years of age.

It was very difficult to locate information relating to Henri Hassler. Fisher (2012) when discussing the New Church establishment in Brisbane mentioned that there was a link between the ornithologist, musician and artist, Sylvester Diggles, the New Church and Henri Hassler.[9] When Diggles conducted the first sacramental service for the New Church in 1866, his friend Henri Hassler was in attendance. Were there any prior links between Hassler and the children of Andrew Graham? Did Hassler actually know the Graham children? How much was received from the 'rents and profits' of Andrew Graham's real estate? The real estate assets of Andrew Graham were the inn locations that had been in Grey and Stanley Streets, South Brisbane.

Additional information was provided (R W Black *Personal Communication* 4 November 2018) relating to Annie Graham. It was pointed out that Annie was named as recipient of dividends from Graham's real estate in 1863:

> (but) in the same year (1863) she married John Cockerill. In 1865 they purchased the licence for the Bowen Hotel from Daniel Donivan who was about to build the Ship Inn just up the street. The Bowen Hotel was formerly known as the Steam

Packet Hotel, and before that was known as the Harp of Erin. It was on the south side of Stanley Street, between Glenelg and Russell Streets. Annie had bought the pub that she grew up in as a small child.

## Reflecting on Hannah and Friends

If Hannah were able to return to South Brisbane during the 2020s, she would be amazed at the population growth, the height of buildings, the number of shops and the speed of buses, trains and planes. Technology has changed much of her South Brisbane. However, it could be the role of women that surprised and pleased her most. Women can now vote in elections, become members of parliament, even premiers or prime ministers. The move toward equality of the sexes has been quite substantial in the past 180 years.

The inaugural ARA Historical Novel Prize ($50,000) was won by Mirandi Riwoe for her novel *Stone Sky Gold Mountain*. *The Australian,* 11 November, 2020 quotes Riwoe as saying 'working-class women, for example, are not represented in our histories'. A reviewer of Riwoe's book, Theresa Smith wrote, 'you really didn't want to be anything other than a white man in 19th century Australia' (*www.theresasmithwrites.com*). There is considerable truth in the comments made by the author and reviewer of *Stone Sky Gold Mountain*. The current book regarding the life of Hannah in colonial Australia is about a working-class woman. If Hannah's experiences in Northern NSW were translated into the language usage of today, the terms sexism, racism, and misogyny would certainly appear.

Hannah arrived in 1842 when Brisbane was little more than a small raw village. She was one of those incredible women who left Ireland as a teenager, arriving in the colony with no support network and probably no money.

Digitised newspapers and archival materials formed the major data sources for this consideration of Hannah and friends. We now know considerably more about these early Australians, but it is inevitable a number of gaps will always exist in their life stories. Photographs and letters are significant in our interpretation of others, but these were not available to assist in putting together our understanding of this interesting woman called Hannah.

The initial image is of a young Irish woman arriving in the very strange and quite confronting British colony of New South Wales. She quickly had responsibilities in the form of children and was frequently required to manage a busy inn. This was quite an incredible achievement in a social setting where male dominance was deeply ingrained.

The sub-tropical climate would have been very demanding on this young Irish woman. Mosquitoes, snakes and the risk of flooding were also realities in her new home. There were issues of personal safety in South Brisbane as a result of the makeup of the new population and the level of disenchantment among the Indigenous landowners.

## Hannah & Friends: Life in South Brisbane

In 1842 when Hannah arrived in Brisbane from Ireland, the population was a few hundred. Census data was collected for Brisbane in the early years, but the boundary defining Brisbane was somewhat flexible. Fisher (2012) quoting from the *New South Wales Government Gazette* 3 November 1846, reported the population was at that time '614 persons in North Brisbane and 346 in South Brisbane'.[10] By 1861 the census set the population figure for Brisbane at 6051. Brisbane was a small isolated town during the time Hannah lived in South Brisbane. There were, of course, a number of Indigenous people in and around the Brisbane settlement during Hannah's early years in the colony. These were not included in early census collections.

Hannah, Andrew Graham, and Frank Mercer lived in a work environment where strict conditions were attached to the granting of a liquor licence. Many of these conditions were in operation as soon as requests had been made to sell alcohol. It was the consolidation of various regulations during the 1860s that finally produced a legal document formalising all conditions relating to gaining a licence and actually running an inn (hotel). In summary, a fee was paid for the licence, and there were conditions regarding cleanliness. The building had to have two moderately sized sitting rooms, and in the case of the *Harp of Erin*, these were described as parlours. In addition to the bedrooms for the licensee and family, two additional bedrooms were required for guests. The availability of stabling and fodder for six horses was also required. The name of the hotel and the licensee had to be displayed in legible letters. A lamp containing two burners must illuminate the sign. Although there were some female innkeepers, it was virtually impossible for a single woman to take on this role. As a widower, the wife of the licensee could take over the licence held by her husband. If the widow remarried while holding the licence for an inn, it was transferred to the new spouse, irrespective of his prior occupation.

The apparently strict regulations for the licensee of an inn seem quite impressive. Unfortunately, between the years 1840 to 1860, when Andrew, Hannah and Frank held alcohol licences, the sly-grog trade was also booming in the Moreton Bay and Darling Downs districts. Newspaper reports state that there were times when the dray owners made the decision to move the very profitable sly grog around, rather than the wool in the Darling Downs sheds.

There is no doubt that Hannah and many of the 'small' early settlers led a tough life. In general, we know very little about the values, personality and interests of such settlers. Hannah demonstrated kindness toward Mrs Jubb as she made her way across the Fassifern. Throughout her life, she displayed an immense capacity to cope with the untimely deaths of her husbands and some of her children. Sadly, coping with the male bias of society was probably seen as a reality of life.

We do know something about the people she lived near or did business with, but to state whether such people were friends is extremely difficult. Hannah did establish strong relationships with relatives from her first marriage to Andrew Graham. Selina Graham, Andrew's sister, was working for Hannah in 1850 at the *Harp of Erin*, or it may have been called the *Steam Packet*

*Inn* by then. John Graham, Hannah's son, was working for her at the *Royal Oak Hotel* in 1859. Annie Graham was working at the *Royal Oak* when the unfortunate Jeremiah Harney incident took place in 1860.

The map in Part 2 of this book names the original owners of allotments in South Brisbane. On the corner of the then-called Stanley and Russell streets was an allotment owned by E Connolly. The owner of this allotment was a neighbour of the Grahams, but initially, no mention could be located regarding this person in the newspapers. A title search conducted by the *Department of Natural Resources, Mapping and Energy* showed that the E stood for Elizabeth, who was the wife of William Connolly. William managed the Hunter River Steam Navigation Company's wharf and the business of the steamers *Tamar* and *Sovereign*. In May 1851 the South Brisbane solicitor John Ocock had the allotment transferred into the names of William Connolly and wife. Later that year, the inn owner on the other side of Stanley Street, John McCabe, purchased the allotment between the years 1853 to 1856. As to what McCabe used that allotment for, no convincing evidence was located. The extent of contact between the Grahams and Elizabeth Connolly is not known.

John Orr and family lived in the same block as Hannah for a number of years and were likely friends. He was a butcher and seemed the obvious supplier of meat for the inn. Jessica, his daughter, was a witness at the wedding between Hannah and Andrew Graham. When Graham was ill and travelled to Sydney with two servants, Jessica Orr also travelled on the steamer, possibly as a helper.

There were other incidents that suggested Hannah and family had links to the Orrs. In 1847 a 'scoundrel' named Samuel Davis endeavoured to burn down the *Harp of Erin*, and members of the Orr family kept a watch on Davis while Graham sought a constable. A decade later, Hannah's second husband, Frank Mercer, witnessed and gave evidence regarding an incident between John Orr and a 'troubled and diminutive celestial' referred to as Champoo.

In 1861 Hannah moved to Ipswich, and in September the same year the *Courier* carried the following advertisement indicating her long-time neighbours, the Orrs, had also moved on.

> Shipping and Family Butcher
>
> WILLIAM BAYNES
>
> (Successor to J and W Orr)
>
> STANLEY QUAY, SOUTH BRISBANE
>
> Vessels supplied punctually by boat to any parts of the river.

Although Hannah moved between her premises in Grey and Stanley Streets, it seems highly probable that considerable opportunity existed for communication to occur between these two families.

There were people like William Sheehan who owned the next-door lot to the Grahams in South Brisbane. He had been the innkeeper of *St Patrick's Hotel* from 1846 to 1848. In 1846 Sheehan sold his allotment in Stanley Street to James Ramsay, a constable. Ramsay remained a constable until September 1849. When the debts of Andrew Graham required assessment in 1849, Hannah had Sheehan approved as one of the assessors. In 1859 when Hannah placed an advertisement in the paper about renting the *Steam Packet Inn,* she asked that enquiries should be made to either her or William Sheehan who had moved to North Brisbane. It would seem that Hannah may have considered Sheehan as a friend. At the least, she kept in touch with Sheehan from the early 1840s to 1859.

William Lacy lived just down the road from the Grahams. Given the small population in the early South Brisbane area, Lacy would have known the Grahams, but whether they were friendly is not known. Lacy did put his name down to join the first volunteer band in South Brisbane: he played the cornopean (cornet). In 1863 Lacy was the assistant boatman pilot for the port of Moreton Bay. An obituary in the *Brisbane Courier* September 1932 for a Mr John Lacy reported that William Lacy had been his father. In this obituary, a comment was made about William Lacy being for 'many years the lighthouse keeper on Moreton Island'. Historic timelines for Moreton Bay Island reported on the web show that between 1848 and 1909, the pilots at Bulwer guided boats into the channel.

William and Margaret Lacy appear to have had every opportunity to get to know Hannah. They remained the owners of their allotment for some years, but it was actually leased to an industrial firm. When William Lacy died in 1874, his allotment was still under the old title system. William named as his executors and trustees, his son Lewis and William Boys. Lewis, who died in 1881, was a mail contractor for the Etheridge area near

Georgetown. The remaining executor, William Boys, signed a declaration in 1877, indicating that the Lacy children had requested him to sell the land. He also had the allotment moved under the 1861 Real Property Act, and in a declaration suggested the allotment was worth £4000. Was this a wishful thinking value?

Hannah and the Orr family lived in Stanley Street for some years. Both left in 1861, Hannah to Ipswich, and the family butcher was taken over by an expanding butchery owed by William Baynes. Hannah could well have been friends with the Orr family.

William Fitzpatrick, the Chief Constable in Brisbane and his wife Mary Anne were witnesses at the wedding between Hannah and Frank Mercer. Hannah also requested that Fitzpatrick be one of the assessors of the *Harp of Erin* debts and thus may have been Hannah's friend.

McCabe was the licensee of the *Commercial Hotel* from 1846 to 1853. This hotel was just across Stanley Street from the Grahams. They would have known McCabe, but as a business competitor he may not have been a close friend. In 1849 McCabe advertised an auction for his block, which was over three acres. This was not the allotment his hotel was on as it was just 36 perches. Using convict labour, the government had previously levelled the acreage block, and it was suggested it would make a good vineyard. The site was portrayed as beautifully situated and it looked over what was described as the 'calm and placid waters of the Brisbane River'. No evidence was located that the proposed sale occurred. This was a good outcome, as it probably saved the potential buyer and his vineyard from being washed into Moreton Bay by the next flood.

John McCabe did own Connolly's old allotment for nearly three years between 1853 and 1856, thus enhancing the possibility of becoming friends with Hannah and her family

John and William Melville had business dealings with Hannah from 1856 to 1859. Initially, this was about renting the *Steam Packet* site as a boarding house, but then as an inn. The Melvilles clearly had discussions with Hannah, but it is not known if they were friends.

Hannah obviously knew Sarah Greenwood, who had been working for her during the 1860 Harney cases, but again, knowing Sarah does not equate with friendship. Sarah was probably a member of the Greenwood family who had a hotel in Grey Street. Paddington Cemetery Records state that Christopher Henry Greenwood died in March 1857 at the age of 23 and that he kept a hotel in Grey Street, near Russell Street in South Brisbane. The *Moreton Bay Courier* reported that the Greenwoods held a hotel in South Brisbane but it was under various names. The fact that there are many gaps in the *Publican's Index NSW Archives* makes it extremely difficult to verify data relating to the Greenwood family in South Brisbane. The *Brisbane Hotels and Publicans Index (1842 to 1900)* lists Edward, James and Mary Greenwood as having liquor licences in this general area. James held the licence for the *Queens Arms* at Kangaroo Point in 1856–57, and Mary held the licence for the *Brisbane Hotel*, South Brisbane in 1858.[11]

Hannah and Frank Mercer were initially friendly with Arthur S Lyon, the newspaper editor, who lived at their inn for nearly a year. This came to an abrupt end when Lyon took Frank Mercer to court in 1853 regarding a dispute over the ownership of a boat.

Hannah would have known a number of lawyers and magistrates as she applied for various liquor licences and also made several appearances in court. When Hannah failed to get a licence in 1861, her legal adviser was Charles Lilley. Hannah knew Lilley as an energetic barrister but had no way of knowing he would go on to be Chief Justice, enter politics, and despite some messy incidents, become the fourth Premier of Queensland. During his extremely busy life in Brisbane, he spent some time as a journalist and newspaper editor and actually purchased a share in the *Moreton Bay Courier*. He was knighted, and the federal seat of Lilley is named after him.

When Fisher (2012) wrote about colonial Brisbane, he noted there were many differences between north and south Brisbane. He also mentioned that 'the vagrants, drunkards, swearers, brawlers and light–fingered gentry' were rather thick on the ground in South Brisbane. There were also some unruly women in the area, in particular, Mary Ann Williams. This interesting, but rather sad woman, frequented the inns and would have been known by Hannah. Unfortunately, she was also disorderly and promiscuous and went to court many times. One night in 1851 she was arrested in South Brisbane, and as there was no lock-up there, the constables took her across the river in the punt. Mary Ann jumped overboard, and the constables had to jump in and pull her on board. News would have travelled fast in a small community. Hannah probably heard about this the next morning and may have felt sorry for Mary Ann. Mr Williams, Mary Ann's husband, had tried to disown her and had moved for a legal settlement, probably experiencing deep despair with respect to her antics.

Working in the bar and serving meals to customers, Hannah must have spoken to hundreds of not only the early South Brisbane arrivals, but also to travellers passing through the area. It is likely that over the years as an innkeeper some of the South Brisbane 'regulars' greeted Hannah as a casual friend.

Andrew Graham knew everybody who counted in Brisbane, and if they could link him to opportunity, he would have 'liked' them. As Frank Mercer ran an inn with Hannah, at both South Brisbane and on the Fassifern, he met many people. It is highly likely that those named as possible friends with Hannah were also his friends.

Those who reflect longingly on the 'good old days' must keep in mind that in the 1840s and 1850s life expectancy was rather short. Andrew Graham was dead at 28, Frank Mercer at 32 and Hannah at 37. Taking a 2020s stance, we would say Andrew, Frank and Hannah died in what should have been the prime of their lives. This was not the case, as their short life expectancy was linked to poor diet, lack of medical knowledge, poor medical facilities and totally inadequate sanitation.

We do not know when Hannah became trapped by alcohol. In the early 1850s Hannah lost two babies at a few weeks of age and a third died at 4-years-old. Her husband Frank became ill and got into debt; by mid-1857 he was insolvent, and by the end of 1857 he had died. Perhaps Hannah's drinking problems were related to these years of abject disaster.

Hannah was married twice and had seven children. At the time of her death, three children were still alive: John Joshua Graham, Andrew Graham (Jnr) and Frank Mercer (Jnr). The number of children Hannah had and the number of children dying was not unusual, as life expectancy and infantile mortality rates were vastly different from those experienced today.

In 1867 the life expectancy in Australian colonies was given as 45.2 years for non-indigenous Australians. Improvements in diet, sanitary conditions and medical knowledge resulted in substantial improvements in life expectancy. The life expectancy for all Australians in 2020 was 81 years (males) and 85 years (females).

Allied to short life expectancy rates was the infantile mortality rate. This rate is for the deaths that occur in the first year of life. Hannah and Andrew Graham had three children. John Joshua Graham was born in 1846 and died at age 83 in 1929. Richard Graham was born in 1847 and lived 11 years. Andrew Hamilton Graham was born in 1848 and died in 1919, aged 71 years. The situation was vastly different regarding Hannah's births during her second marriage to Frank Mercer. Sarah Campbell Mercer was born 4 April 1851 but perished during a flood 8 February 1855. She had not reached the age of four. In addition to this, the *Moreton Bay Courier* reported the death of Louisa Ann Mercer in August 1852 and stated that her short life had lasted 10 weeks. In June 1853 Louisa Anna's death was reported. She lived for eight days. These must have been horrendous times for Hannah and Frank Mercer. Their last child was a son named Frank Dawson Mercer. He was born in 1857 and died in 1891, thus living 34 years.

Part of Hannah's life was involved in legal cases. She was twice called as a witness in murder trials. In both instances the accused had been drinking at her inn. The first case was in 1849 when Owen Molloy was found guilty of murder, and the second was in 1854 when John Hanley was found guilty of murder. Surprisingly, in the latter's case, the death sentence was reduced to five years hard labour. In July 1854 the *Moreton Bay Courier* expressed its outrage at this decision. It was the paper's view that Hanley had committed a murder, and yet he received a punishment that was more appropriate 'in a petty case of dishonesty'.

Assessing how busy the Grahams were at their inns in Grey and Stanley Streets is extremely complex. The amount of liquor ordered from Sydney provides some indication of the size of their trade. Perhaps the fact that Andrew or Hannah held licences in the same area from 1843 to 1859 is an indication of their success. Many of the inns in Brisbane changed their licensee regularly and often went out of business quickly. There is no way of reporting how often and for what length of time clients sought to be accommodated at these

South Brisbane inns. We do know that three of the longer term clients ended their association with these inns on most unpleasant terms. Andrew Graham, in 1847, clashed with the showman George Croft over an accommodation account. Frank Mercer and Arthur Lyon ended up in court in an 1853 dispute over a boat and apparent costs arising out of accommodation at the inn. During 1860 Hannah Mercer was involved in two legal actions involving Jeremiah Harney, who had been living at the inn for over four weeks. These disputes focussed on the ownership of a horse, documentary accuracy, accommodation, alcohol and mental stability.

When Hannah's first husband, Andrew Graham, died in late 1848, she was involved for some months in an 'affidavits battle' to reverse key components of Andrew's will and thus provide her with control of his assets. The will had also given guardianship of the children to persons other than Hannah. This was reversed during the 'affidavits battle'.

It is assumed that the will Andrew Graham made in Sydney was a personal blow to Hannah. Hannah's legal action relating to Andrew's will revealed financial data that was probably another blow for Hannah. Over a period of six years, it seems that the inn had accumulated enormous bar debts of almost £400. Hannah may have been the person who did the work at the inn, but in a male dominated society it would be no surprise if Andrew was in charge of money matters.

Inns, or as they became known, hotels, have always been the setting for discussions relating to the local gossip and scandals. In the first half of 1849, Hannah was involved

## Hannah & Friends: Life in South Brisbane

in a legal battle to reverse the seemingly unfair clauses of Andrew's will. Was this a topic for discussion among the 'regulars' at her inn? At the same time this legal battle was occurring, Wickham was endeavouring to make sense as to how the *Fortitude,* with her assisted immigrants, managed to arrive in Moreton Bay with apparently no appropriate arrangements made by Dunmore Lang. These arrivals were eventually 'shovelled' down the hill into Fortitude Valley. Perhaps this was the topic of discussion among all 'regulars' at Brisbane inns.[12]

It is extremely likely that two court cases in 1860 were personally demanding and probably did considerable damage to Hannah's standing in the Brisbane community. These cases focussed on the ownership of a horse. Other variables such as alcoholism, document credibility and the validity of witness statements, were raised during the cases or court proceedings. Jeremiah Harney was a key person in these cases. It was noted that six years prior to the 1860 cases, he had been involved in another 'horse case' and the judge queried his mental capacities. These cases kept Hannah's name in the newspaper and inevitably innuendo would have arisen. The next year her application for a liquor licence was rejected.

Hannah lived in the South Brisbane region for approximately 18 years, and at both the *Bush Inn* in the Fassifern area, and Ipswich for nearly two years. There is no evidence regarding her health at South Brisbane. Nor is there any evidence as to whether she appointed a housekeeper following the advertisement in 1860. Perhaps she knew it might be difficult obtaining a liquor licence in Brisbane and hence the comment in the advertisement about the successful applicant for the position of housekeeper may need to move to the country.

The majority of the population, including Hannah, experienced 'tough lives'. This was probably more so for women than men. There are many questions we would have liked to ask Hannah. She left Ireland as a teenager and no evidence could be located that she ever had contact again with relatives in Ireland. Her life in South Brisbane and Ipswich was obviously demanding. We can but wonder regarding the extent she reflected upon what her life would have been like in Cork during the famine period. Given that she had never experienced anything like gender equity, it is highly likely that such an issue did not impinge on her short hard-working life. To those who may reflect on the life of Hannah, we can hope she experienced periods of joy and happiness while living in the then small and raw townships of South Brisbane and Ipswich.

## *Final Snapshot of Hannah*

Hannah arrived in the colony of NSW as an entry on the log of a sailing ship. This entry could well have consigned her to obscurity, in what for years was a penal colony. She arrived as a working-class girl. Initially, she could read but not write, but she had the drive and determination to become a businesswoman. This was an incredible achievement in a society dominated by a belief in male superiority.

We now know much more about Hannah and believe she had a rather high profile in the area she lived. Her first husband, Andrew, may have purchased what became the locations for the inns, but Hannah was the stabilising influence at the inns in South Brisbane. Andrew seemed to be more interested in fraternising with high-profile members of society and supporting charitable groups than the demands associated with running an inn. Hannah's second husband, Frank, had attended an elite school in London, but by the time he left England it seemed that he was in considerable debt. He had communicated with his father, Reverend Mercer, and given him the impression that he had experienced considerable success in the colony. He did gain a licence for an inn, but he had a substantial interest in horse racing. He eventually became insolvent, and Hannah raised funds to cover his debts. As a horse-racing man, Mercer may well have put strain on the inns' finances he and Hannah were associated with.

Inns such as the *Harp of Erin* were a short walk away from where the sailing ships tied up, and it is easy to imagine what life was like for people such as Hannah when the crews from these ships 'hit the inns' on shore.

During the period of Hannah's life in the South Brisbane area, it was rather unusual for a woman to appear in court. This was not true of Hannah, as she had to fight for her rights and defend herself against charges associated with business. Hannah had dealings with the high-profile Brisbane lawyers.

Like so many other women at the time, Hannah experienced the loss of children and the untimely deaths of husbands. Like so many other inn licensees, this incredible woman died an alcoholic.

# Hannah's Timeline

| | |
|---|---|
| 1825 | Born in Cork, baptised in Killarney. |
| 1840 | Leaves Ireland. |
| 1841 | Arrived in colony of NSW. |
| 1842 | Makes her way to Brisbane. |
| 1845 | Marries Andrew Graham and lives at Harp of Erin Inn. |
| 1848 | Andrew dies of tuberculosis in Sydney. |
| 1849 | Challenges Andrew's will. |
| 1849 | Hannah now has 3 children and a step daughter to care for, and the Harp of Erin Inn to run. |
| 1849 | Changes inn name to Steam Packet Hotel. |
| 1851 | Marries Frank Mercer. |
| 1853 | Frank has dispute with Arthur Lyon. |
| 1854 | Frank's application for Brisbane inn licence rejected. |

| | |
|---|---|
| **1854** | Frank and Hannah move to Bush Inn, Fassifern. |
| **1854-57** | Death of three children. Frank becomes ill, insolvent and dies. |
| **1859** | Hannah reopens the Royal Oak Hotel. |
| **1859** | Melville's rent Steam Packet site. |
| **1860** | Two court cases involving Jeremiah Harney. |
| **1861** | Hannah's licence application rejected in Brisbane. |
| **1861** | Hannah obtains licence in Ipswich. |
| **1862** | Hannah dies at Union Hotel (One-Mile Creek), Ipswich. |

# Part 2
# Hannah and her Neighbours

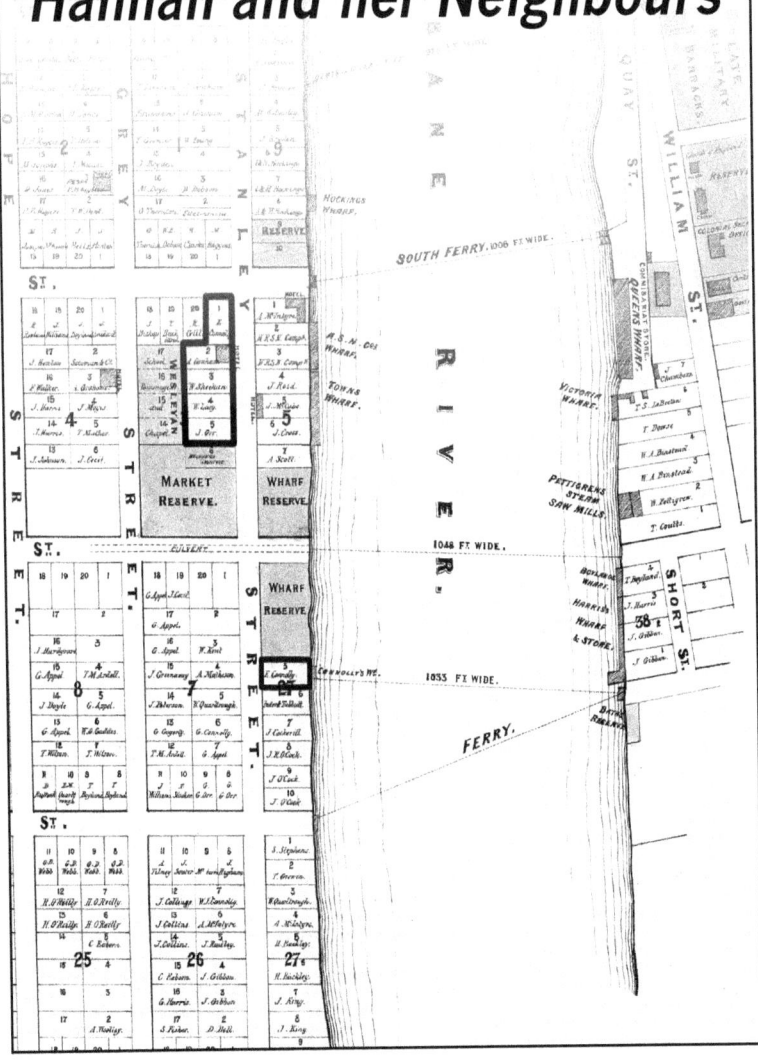

## Background

This section of the book has as its focus a microanalysis of the early settlers who occupied five South Brisbane allotments between the years 1843 into the 1870s. Each of the allotments selected was close to Graham's Inn (Lot 2). In simple terms, the idea was to describe who initially purchased these allotments and who then owned or occupied them for the next 30 years or so. These allotments commenced at the corner of Russell and Stanley streets and ran down the then-called Stanley Street in a south-easterly direction.[13]

Details of these allotments and their owners were taken from the initial title deeds and are detailed below.[14] *Ham's Map of the City of Brisbane* (1863) shows allotment 1 to 5 in Section 3 and a second purchase by Elizabeth Connolly, Lot 5, Section 6, South Brisbane.

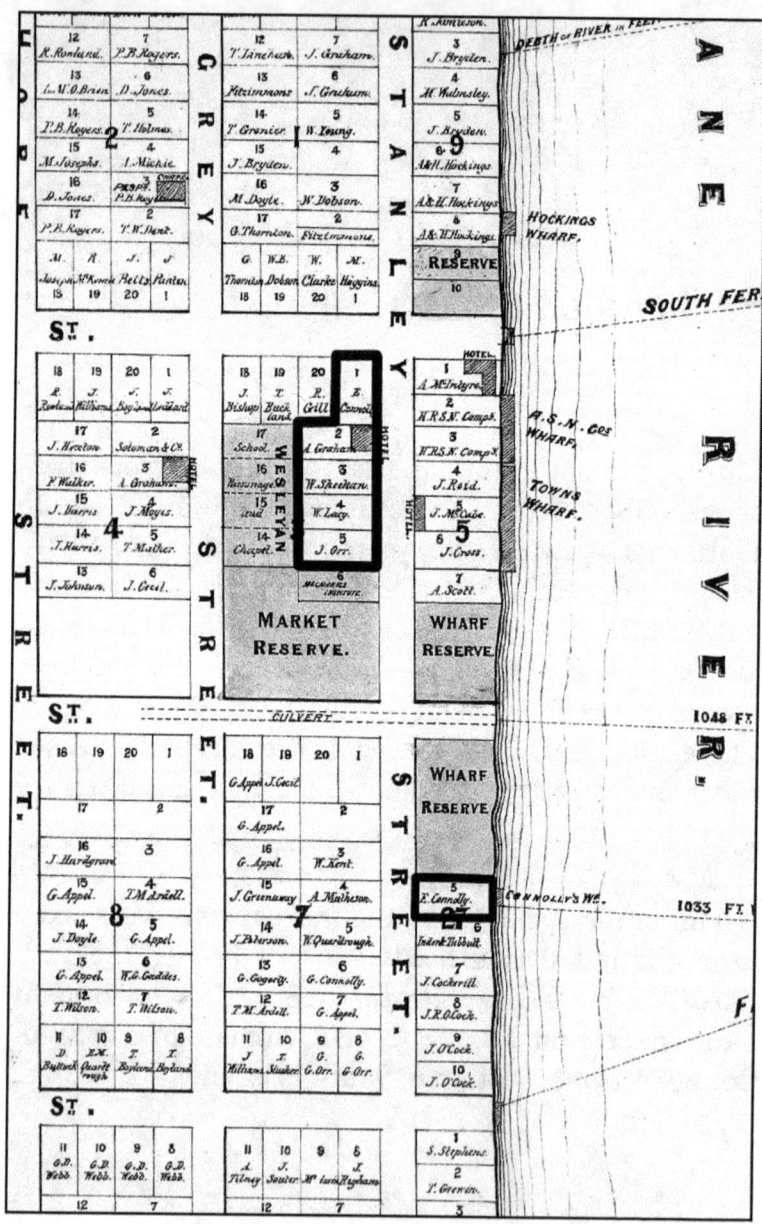

8. Allotment 1 to 5 in Section 3 and allotment 5, Section 6, South Brisbane

## Hannah & Friends: Life in South Brisbane

| Owner | Allotment |
|---|---|
| Elizabeth Connolly | Lot 1 Section 3 South Brisbane: 36 Perches: Price 22/10/- |
| Andrew Graham | Lot 2 Section 3 South Brisbane: 36 Perches: Price £29/14/- |
| William Sheehan | Lot 3 Section 3 South Brisbane: 36 Perches: Price £26/02/- |
| William Lacy | Lot 4 Section 3 South Brisbane: 36 Perches: Price £22/10/- |
| John Orr | Lot 5 Section 3 South Brisbane: 36 Perches: Price £22/10/- |

The decision to withdraw convicts from the Moreton Bay and Darling Downs districts of New South Wales (NSW) in 1839 immediately created labour shortages in the rural areas of the colony and the small northern townships such as Ipswich and Brisbane. Development was urgently needed in the rough-and-ready townships and one of the consequences that arose was the commencement of land sales in the townships from 1842.

In 1843 Andrew Graham began operating the *Harp of Erin Inn* at Grey Street, South Brisbane. By 1845 Hannah Sweeny had become Hannah Graham, and she began work at the inn. Hannah, apart from becoming a wife, helped Andrew overcome the labour shortage and became a mother for Andrew's daughter Annie.

South Brisbane, where the Grahams lived, was viewed as a unique section of the Brisbane township and various authors, travellers and settlers commented on this uniqueness.

Rod Fisher (2012) wrote about the two very differing towns in colonial Brisbane. Although only divided by a river, Fisher noted the rather sharp contrasts between North and South Brisbane. He commented about South Brisbane having rather temporary wooden houses, many small inns, a rustic feel and more evidence of minority groups. Fisher drew attention to the number of unruly women in South Brisbane and, as mentioned earlier, he believed that this area contained 'more vagrants, drunkards, swearers and light-fingered gentry than elsewhere'.

When writing for the *Queenslander* in 1915, William Clark (1837-1918) stated that when Thomas Archer's wool drays travelled from various stations on the Darling Downs in 1841, there was hardly a house in South Brisbane.[15] Thomas Archer and his brothers from Scotland took up large pastoral properties in the Moreton Bay District, including Durundur. This 200 square mile station was centred on the now town of Woodford. Thomas Archer became Agent General for Queensland in the late 1800s. William Clark arrived in Brisbane in 1849 and his obituary in 1918 noted that he was a valued contributor to the *Courier* and *Queenslander* for many years. He had considerable experience in the pastoral industry, including an involvement in the driving of stock from Coopers Plains to Camboon Station on the Dawson River for James Reid. Reid, an early Queensland settler, owned a riverside allotment on Stanley Street, directly opposite the five allotments under consideration in this book.

## Hannah & Friends: Life in South Brisbane

In 1853 Chas Melton arrived in Brisbane and initially lived in South Brisbane. Melton worked for the *Courier* for 50 years and in April 1918 presented a paper to the Historical Society of Queensland. In this paper, Melton mentioned the wide open spaces and noted that a large salt water creek wended its way between Stanley and Grey streets before entering the river just below John Orr's butchery.[16]

Nehemiah Bartley made his first trip to Brisbane in 1854. Bartley was Queensland's first commercial traveller, agent for everything, and a prodigious note-taker. He wrote the 'muddy brackish water which separates north from south Brisbane marked the boundary of two townships so closely dissimilar in all aspects' (p.250). South Brisbane reminded Bartley of the rural outback, but North Brisbane was more 'finicky'.[17]

Alcohol forms a strong thread running through the history of remote and isolated settlements in the colony of NSW. Inns were approved rather rapidly as the fees from licences improved the coffers of NSW authorities. It is no surprise that there was an illegal trade in alcoholic beverages. These sly groggers could set up their illegal stills to tempt the local inhabitants, or alternatively, they could buy and 'sell on' these elixirs of promised delight. South Brisbane was not devoid of those described as 'sly groggers' and innkeepers such as the Grahams and William Sheehan would have preferred to see an end to this trade.

In October 1843 John C Wickham, the then Police Magistrate, placed an advertisement in the *Moreton Bay*

*Courier* regarding the convict James Bennett. Bennett was charged with committing a crime in NSW, but while awaiting trial, he escaped goal.

The *Moreton Bay Courier* in July 1846 became irritated by the antics of the escapee. The paper claimed that Bennett made weekly nocturnal visits to his supplier in South Brisbane, and this he sold to the hut keepers on the Albert and Logan rivers. The rum was sold at eight shillings a quart and this apparently represented a substantial profit. The newspaper suggested he carried out his trade in a most bare-faced manner and that surely the town constables and border police knew about Bennett. No information was obtained relating to the arrest of Bennett.

## Lot 1 Elizabeth Connolly

E Connolly was the first owner of Lot 1 and it was not until the allotment titles were obtained that it became known that the owner's first name was Elizabeth and that she was married to William Connolly.

There may be an interesting story behind how and why this woman became an allotment owner, but it is currently obscured from this author. In the early 1840s colonial NSW, like much of the world, had an entrenched male-dominated society. There was a place for women, but it was not often associated with land purchase. When Elizabeth purchased Lot 1, the formal witness to the transaction was Sir Charles FitzRoy, Governor of NSW.

Initially, William Connolly was the manager of the Hunter River and Steamship Navigation Company's wharf. He handled the bookings for the *Tamar* and *Sovereign* steamers and later reports in the *Moreton Bay Courier* indicate that Connolly became a general agent between 1846 and 1850. He advertised rental properties, including a sheep station. Connolly became involved in managing the affairs of an insolvent settler, acting as a debt collector, and in 1849 he endeavoured to organise a program for the importation of Chinese labourers.

In March 1849 Elizabeth Connolly purchased another allotment in South Brisbane. This was Allotment 5, Section 6, 37 perches, at a cost of £23 2s 6d.

There was a reconveyance with respect to the title of Connolly's Lot 1, Section 3, in May 1851. A reconveyance is the transfer of a title to the borrower after the mortgage has been paid in full.

The front page of the Lot 1 reconveyance document reads 'John Ocock, Gent, to Mr William Connolly'. It seemed that John Ocock had gained the ownership of Lot 1. Within the document, it is recorded Connolly paid £50 to Ocock in order to retain the title deeds to Lot 1. Ocock was an early, and very active, barrister in South Brisbane. Although Elizabeth Connolly was noted as the owner of Lot 1, it was clearly legal for an allotment to be in the name of the wife but for the husband to make legal decisions relating to the allotment.

On 20 December 1851, seven months after the involvement of Ocock in Lot 1, the owners of the allotment were described as being William Connolly and wife. These owners of Lot 1 sold the allotment to John McCabe, a licensed victualler. McCabe does not appear in the textbooks as a significant figure in early Brisbane history, but there is no doubt he was a 'doer' and the type of early settler with commercial foresight who contributed to the expansion of the embryonic colony.

One of the first steps toward establishing a more efficient legal system in the northern districts of NSW was to ensure that suitable jurors were available. In

October 1850 a list of such persons was compiled and McCabe was on the list. McCabe held the licence of the *Commercial Hotel* until 1856. This hotel was on the river side of Stanley Street, approximately 150 metres from Lot 1 (see Fig.8). No precise information could be located regarding the activities John McCabe carried out from Lot 1 during 1852 and 1853. This is a surprise as the reading of newspaper entries tends to suggest McCabe was the type of early South Brisbane settler who was mentioned in the *Moreton Bay Courier*, even if he just submitted a letter to the editor.

A selection of these entries informs the reader that McCabe had some difficulties with the quality of labour employed at the hotel. In 1847 he brought a charge against Joseph Crawford for absconding from his hired service position and in 1850, his hired servant, David Way, was charged with being a habitual drunk, abusive and lazy. Both received prison sentences.

Perhaps there were only a few well-watered paddocks in South Brisbane, causing McCabe in 1848 and 1850 to warn the public of prosecution if a particular South Brisbane paddock was used without his permission. This paddock was strictly reserved for the use of his customers. In 1848 McCabe purchased an allotment in Ipswich, reported on the refurbishment of the *Commercial Hotel* in 1849, and in 1850 offered a reward for his horse which had strayed in the Woogaroo area.

In 1849 McCabe advertised his nearby three acre block that had been previously levelled by convict labour as an ideal site for a vineyard. It was stated that this site overlooked 'the calm and placid waters of the Brisbane River'. This was hardly an accurate description of a river which had a history of flooding. No evidence of a sale was noted that year.

Not all McCabe's notations in newspapers were associated with joy and happiness among his South Brisbane neighbours. In June 1850 John McCabe left the *Commercial Hotel* without tying up his dog. He returned to find the dog had bitten the daughter of Thomas Grenier, the nearby proprietor of the *Brisbane Hotel* in Russell Street. Grenier demanded the dog be put down. McCabe, in a letter to the editor of the *Moreton Bay Courier* said, he had told Grenier the dog was very important and that he would cover all expenses if the dog was not destroyed. He believed that an agreement had been reached. The next time McCabe went out, the dog was chained up. He returned to find that Grenier had arrived and shot the dog.

Thomas and Mary Grenier spent 1832-34 in America but moved to New Zealand. In 1841 they arrived in Brisbane where Thomas opened a butcher's shop in Queen Street but soon moved to South Brisbane as he obtained the licence for the *Brisbane Hotel*. The social authority on everything, Nehemiah Bartley, frequented this hotel and believed it was the best in Brisbane. Grenier continued to purchase various sections of land and his most successful acquisition was the 640 acre Portion 18, Yeerongpilly.

In December 1854 the *Moreton Bay Courier* reported another distressing incident for McCabe. An intruder maliciously stabbed McCabe's valuable horse to death during the night. At that time, horses were the essential means of moving around and as a consequence could be treated with greater respect than some of the citizens. McCabe offered a £100 reward for the identification of the intruder. The vicious destruction of the horse resulted in 115 angry people contributing donations toward the reward. The names on the list read like a who's who of significant early settlers in Brisbane. The final reward figure advertised was £530/11/-, but no evidence of a conviction was noted.

The sale of Lot 1 to McCabe was not a simple legal transaction. The first component of the deed of conveyance relates to a legal agreement reached between William and Elizabeth Connolly and the trustees of the Moreton Bay Benefit Investment and Building Society. The trustees were three extremely influential and well-respected people in the Moreton Bay District. These were William Hobbs, a highly regarded medical man, Robert Little, a solicitor and investor who became the Crown Solicitor, and John Richardson, who was involved in various commercial activities in the township but was also a pastoralist and parliamentarian. The document states that 'the trustees will provide the sum of ninety pounds to the said William Connolly at the request of Elizabeth Connolly'. This 'advance' was paid from the funds of the particular Moreton Bay Society. The title document then goes on to indicate that trustees could now determine the use of the allotment.

For a lay-person, the early deed of conveyance document is difficult to interpret, but it seems that John McCabe agreed to purchase Lot 1 for £20 but in addition was responsible for the repayment of the advance made by the trustees.

This was not the absolute resolution of the conveyance regarding the sale of Lot 1. In what must have been an embarrassing and undignifying experience, William Anthony Brown, a Commissioner of the Supreme Court, called Elizabeth Connolly in for questioning. In response to his major question, Connolly declared that she had executed the document freely and voluntarily, without menace or coercion from her husband or any other person.

McCabe owned property and ran a successful hotel that was periodically expanded. He had purchased Lot 1 for what seemed to be a low price (£110) and sold it for an excellent price (£550). In other words, McCabe had made a shrewd investment. The sale was described as being to a Sydney mariner named Roger Elliott, who was a successful Sydney whaler.

There is no doubt that McCabe was an interesting man. By 1856 he had commenced a general store and wine and spirits outlet in George Street, North Brisbane. In 1859 he was involved in a Supreme Court case with Mrs Catherine Goode regarding financial matters of the legendary *Burnett Inn* at Nanango.

The newspapers contain quite an amount of information regarding McCabe. As an innkeeper, he advertised the *Commercial* in South Brisbane. On moving to George Street in North Brisbane, he continued to advertise his products and was not averse to embracing popular trends. An example being, when dugong oil began appearing for sale, he quickly advertised in the *Moreton Bay Courier* (February 1859) reporting that he had dugong oil 'for both local use and export'.

In September 1854 McCabe placed an advertisement in the *Moreton Bay Courier* which suggested he was not without humour. The advertisement was for two fully equipped and lined marquees. One was 80 feet (24.38m) by 69 feet (21.03m) and the other 24 feet (7.43m) by 18 feet (5.49m). A comment in the advertisement raised the idea of the suitability of the marquees for someone wishing to commence a settlement at Sandgate.

Initially, McCabe lived at the *Commercial Hotel*, but he moved to North Brisbane to live at his George Street business. While running his business in North Brisbane, he continued to own and operate the wharf in front of the *Commercial Hotel*. This hotel was owned by John Campbell from August 1853, but by October 1856 it had been purchased by John Souter. Souter had modernised the hotel and extended it to take over the building owned by James Reid.

McCabe died at age 53 in 1861 and was buried in the Catholic section of the Paddington cemetery. Paddington cemetery records relating to the pioneers of early Brisbane suggest that McCabe was:

> one of the leading merchants at that time, and also owned a number of teams. He also owned Queen's Wharf and a large area of South Brisbane[18]

Brisbane's population growth was on the move by the end of 1853. Assisted immigration schemes were bringing in people mainly of British origin. Dunmore Lang was in the process of arranging ships to arrive with their 'Christian cargo' on board to ensure 'Cooksland' became the type of country Lang thought was appropriate for this new colony. There were opportunists who had heard, or read about, the potential for investment and financial gain in the northern districts of NSW.

In February 1856 Elliott was named on the list of electors as a freeholder in Stanley Street, South Brisbane. When Elliott sold Lot 1 in August 1856, he was still described as a person from the 'City of Sydney' but not as a mariner. He was now identified as a gentleman.

Roger Elliott was actually Captain Elliott of the *Proteus*, a 254 ton barque. The *Proteus* was a sperm oil whaler from 1842 to 1849, and in November 1849 Elliott became the joint owner of this sailing vessel. Sperm oil collection was one of the most profitable early industries in NSW. This oil was initially the primary machine lubricant and the preferred lamp oil in both Europe and North America. In the 1840s fever was a constant problem during sea voyages and the sperm oil was frequently collected in dangerous ocean areas. When the *Proteus* returned to Sydney in 1842, the then captain, first mate, second mate and seven crew members had died from fever.

In 1847 the *Proteus* had been at sea for 23 months and returned to Sydney with a productive cargo of 1100 barrels of oil. A month after returning from this mammoth trip, Richard Elliott was married by special licence to Eliza Lucy Miller in St James Church, Brisbane. The wedding announcement describes Elliott as 'Commander of the *Proteus*', which sounds more significant than Captain.

The special licence may have arisen as a consequence of one of the applicants not being a member of the faith associated with the particular church.

In the early 1850s the 'shipping intelligence' section of the *Moreton Bay Courier* reported that Roger Elliott, now master of the *Zoom*, a two-masted sailing vessel, made a number of trips from Brisbane to Sydney and Melbourne. The *Zoom* was a combined passenger and freight vessel and made various trips in 1852, 1853 and 1854. It is interesting to note that bookings on the *Zoom* were made through William Connolly.

Having paid £550 for Lot 1 in 1856, Elliott sold to Robert Towns for £350/-/-. This seemed like quite a loss, but no additional information was located to explain this outcome. Elliott was initially described as a mariner and this term could have applied to Towns in his early days.

Robert Towns received a meagre elementary education in England, but whilst apprenticed to the master of a collier, he studied at night acquiring the skills of navigation and thus began a career as a mariner. He first went to Sydney in 1823 and eventually became highly successful in commercial activities. Towns owned ships, had links to some of the most powerful international entrepreneurs in the world and formed partnerships with successful traders such as Sir Alexander Stuart. Town's first advertisement in Brisbane appeared in the *Moreton Bay Courier* in 1855. This advertisement reported that as from 15 May 1855, R Towns & Co had for sale: tea, sugar, brandy, rum, port, sherry, woolpacks, rock salt, boots and shoes and window panes. The name of Towns quickly became significant in the Moreton Bay District

9. Portrait of Robert Towns (artist unknown)

as he imported a wide range of products. The *Moreton Bay Courier* reported that for one order in 1857, Towns had delivered 50 bags of flour, 20 hogs heads of beer, 150 barrels of beer, 705 bags of salt and 22 unspecified packages.

Towns took up land on the Darling Downs and along the Brisbane and Logan rivers. The article on Robert Towns (1794-1873) in the *Australian Dictionary of Biography* draws attention to Towns' enormous land holdings in north Queensland. By 1867 he held 42 runs in the North and South Kennedy districts, 94 runs in the Burke District and 60 in the Warrego District. These holdings amounted to over 7,000 square kilometres, and a considerable proportion was held in partnership agreements.

A major development site for Towns was Cleveland Bay in North Queensland. This activity was closely linked with the naming of Townsville and eventually with the erection of a statue of Robert Towns on the city's Pioneers Walk. In July 2020 during the unrest relating to the *Black Lives Matter* movement, graffiti was placed on the Robert Towns statue.

Towns with his 'shipping power' carried many South Sea Island labourers to Queensland. These were referred to as 'Kanakas', a Hawaiian word meaning man. Such activities became known as 'blackbirding', and in many instances this amounted to the virtual enslavement of South Pacific Islanders by force and deception. These Islanders were poorly paid and tended to be put to work in areas associated with cotton and sugar. Robert Towns died in Sydney in 1873 and his trustees sold Lot 1 Section 3, South Brisbane in 1875. Clearly Connolly's original allotment had been an important site for Towns as he held it for 19 years.

In 1875, two years after the death of Towns, his trustees sold Lot 1 to Henry Lock for £975. The Thom Blake's

10. Statue of Robert Towns in Townsville

technique for assessing the change in monetary value was used. The £975 price is estimated to be well over £135,000 in 2021. This is an increase of 135 times since 1875. The major advantage associated with Lot 1 was that it was on a thoroughfare that was a direct link to Logan, Ipswich and the Darling Downs. To this must be added, the ferries and wharves providing the potential to be involved in local, national and international trade. Indeed, at this time many thought that South Brisbane could well become the major focal point of Brisbane.

The only information located regarding Henry Lock was that he held the licence for the *Royal Hotel* between 1875 and 1880. The lack of detail relating to the buyer Lock is more than made up by the details of Robert Towns' trustees who facilitated the sale. The trustees were described on the title deed as Alexander Stuart, a Sydney merchant, George King of Gowrie near Toowoomba, a grazier, Edward Knox Esquire of Sydney and Sophia Towns, Robert Town's widow. Each of the trustees were prominent business people, especially in banking and pastoral activities.

Sophia Towns, wife of Robert Towns, was the half-sister of the extremely influential William Charles Wentworth. Towns, a person with considerable interest in the acquisition of money, began a legal feud with Wentworth. The focus of this feud was the sharing of D'Arcy Wentworth's wealth. Towns believed that Sophia should have received more from D'Arcy's estate and he expended a considerable sum in this failed feud.

Henry Lock, the owner of Lot 1, sold the allotment to John Hardgrave for £420 in April 1879. The initial page of the conveyance document reports that a mortgage was involved, and that Lock had borrowed £900 from Charles Watson of Brisbane at 8%. There were various persons named Watson at this time, but the author's searches did not locate a person who seemed to have the resources to provide a loan of £900.

In November 1906 *The Week* announced the death of John Hardgrave at age 81. Hardgrave was born in Wicklow, Ireland, and came out to Sydney in 1843 and 5 years later moved to Brisbane. In the 1840s he owned a house in North Brisbane, was on the electoral roll, and obtained leather from Sydney to establish a shop in Queen Street. One source indicates that Hardgrave sold boots and shoes and another describes his shop as being involved in the sale of Wellington boots. It is suggested that Hardgrave invested wisely and made a lot of money. It is not clear what his investments were, but after five or six years, he was able to retire. He became Mayor of Brisbane in 1868 and 1869.

## *Title Deed Changes – Lot 1*

| | |
|---|---|
| 1843 | Elizabeth Connolly |
| 1851 | John Ocock |
| 1851 | William Connolly and wife, Elizabeth |
| 1851 | John McCabe |
| 1853 | Roger Elliott |
| 1856 | Robert Towns |
| 1875 | Henry Lock |
| 1879 | John Hardgrave |

## Lot 5 Section 6 Elizabeth Connolly

This allotment is outside those initially identified for consideration in this study. As it was purchased by Elizabeth Connolly on 8 August 1848, it has the potential to increase our understanding of the lives of Elizabeth and William Connolly. It was 37 perches in size and cost Elizabeth £23 2s 6d. There was a small wharf adjacent to this allotment named Connolly's Wharf. It is noted that John Cockerill, who married into the Graham family, owned a nearby allotment and the barrister, John Ocock, owned three allotments in the same location.

William Connolly sold this allotment to Jacob Levi Montefiore and Robert Graham for £230 in January of 1852. Montefiore held this allotment for 14½ years. The *Evening News* in March 1885 commented on the death of Montefiore indicating that he had lived in Sydney for nearly 50 years. He was initially a pastoralist, but his reputation was largely built around his trading activities as the senior partner in Montefiore and Graham and later as Montefiore and Jacob. Montefiore became a magistrate and parliamentarian in Sydney and was

11. Portrait of Jacob Montefiore (1885) by B S Marks

extensively involved in the public life of that city. His trading activities were associated with many parts of the world.

Jacob Montefiore had purchased an allotment in South Brisbane and developed a trading base there, but as mentioned above, he had a substantial involvement in Sydney. This wealthy trader was also involved in South Australia and became one of the South Australian Colonisation Commissioners (1834). He had strong links to Colonel William Light, who selected the site for Adelaide and drew up a street plan.

Other owners of this Connolly allotment included John William Davies, a surgeon who returned to Redditch in England, and Peter Hartley, who worked in Customs but also owned a number of properties.

In November 1862 William Connolly, aged 40, died from bronchitis. At that time, he was a clerk in Customs.

In August of 1871 there was a query regarding a legal document that had been earlier signed by Connolly. Thomas Dowse (Old Tom), describing himself as a commission agent, signed a declaration that he had frequently observed Connolly's writing, and there was no doubt the document had been signed by William Connolly.

John William Davies, the surgeon, sold Allotment 5 Section 6 to Peter Hartley and returned to England. As a consequence there was a need to verify his signature in 1868. In March 1868 Richard Fitzgerald Phelan, an accountant, stated that he was well acquainted with the signature of Davies and could verify the signature in question. Francis Gill in April 1868, a clerk in the Civil Service, made a similar declaration about Davies' signature to Phelan based on his period of service at the Government Savings Bank.

The Connollys had purchased two blocks in South Brisbane and both were eventually owned for some years by highly successful international traders namely, Robert Towns and Jacob Levi Montefiore.

## Lot 2 Andrew Graham

Andrew Graham was from Londonderry, Ireland. His father was a soldier, but Andrew also had considerable exposure to his uncle Reverend John Graham, who was initially a Catholic but recanted and published what some described as 'anti-Popery doggerel'. Andrew and his wife (nee Catherine Knox) left Ireland in 1840 on an assisted immigration scheme for the colony of New South Wales. In their application, they were described as Protestants. These statements were a little from the truth, as Andrew was not married to Catherine, but married couples received more financial support than single people. The other slight error was that Catherine was a Catholic.

When Andrew purchased Lot 2, the official witness on the title document was Sir Charles FitzRoy, Governor of NSW. The lead in for the signature of the witness was presented in the following manner:

*'WITNESS our Trusty and Well-beloved'*
(Space for signature)

Such a formal statement on a legal document would now be considered rather strange.

Andrew and Catherine did marry in 1841 at Raymond Terrace in the lower Hunter River. A baby daughter Ann, but usually called Annie, was born at nearby Morpeth. The Grahams moved to Brisbane, but Catherine died in January 1845. In March of 1845 Andrew married Hannah Sweeny who was a rather new arrival from Ireland.

Andrew had received a liquor licence for an inn on Lot 2 Section 3 in 1843. He called the inn *Harp of Erin*. He was an 'on the go' person who was involved as a member of several early Brisbane committees and agencies. One of his major money-making activities was associated with attracting shepherds for employment by Darling Downs pastoralists.

Perhaps it is an uncharitable view, but Andrew could now follow his various interests as he had Hannah to look after the inn and his baby. Unfortunately, Andrew developed consumption and died in late 1848 at the age of 28 years. Death at such an early age was entirely in-keeping with life expectancy in the mid-1800s.

The title office records indicate that Lot 2, Andrew Graham's initial purchase in Stanley Street, was sold on 7 October 1870. The sellers were John Joshua Alexander Graham, a stockman from Logan River, John Cockerill described as a grazier on the Logan River and his wife Annie Cockerill, and Thomas Shuttler, a farmer from Brisbane. The buyer was Azariah Purchase, a publican from Brisbane.

Two of those identified as sellers of Lot 2 were the children of Andrew Graham. John Graham was the son of Andrew and his second wife Hannah, and Annie Cockerill was the daughter of Andrew and his first wife Catherine. John Cockerill became part of the selling group as he married Annie Graham.

Thomas Shuttler was not part of the Graham family, but may have become a part-owner of Lot 2 as a consequence of a partnership with John Cockerill. Shuttler is described as a Brisbane farmer in the sale document, but there is evidence that he had been a butcher. He may well have been the Thomas Shuttler who in 1858 was a butcher at East Ballarat, Victoria.[19]

In 1861 a Thomas Shuttler of Queen Street, Brisbane, placed an advertisement in the *Courier* 'for a respectable middle-aged female to attend upon a sick lady' but there is no mention of a butcher's shop until September 1862.

An advertisement in September 1862 states that Mr G Orr was about to relinquish his butcher's shop in Stanley Street, South Brisbane, and requested a continuance of his customer's favours for his successors, Messers Cockerill and Shuttler. The shop owned by Mr G Orr was on the corner of Stanley and Ernest streets, a block further up the river from the shop owned by John Orr who usually operated under the name of J and W Orr.

The *Courier* reported in 1862 that Cockerill and Shuttler wanted to employ two men for a fencing job in Stanley Street. In March 1863 they advertised a bull for sale; in June, 250 heavyweight hides were offered for sale; in July, 100 pigs were put up for sale. On 24 July their South Brisbane butcher's shop was advertised for sale or lease. During 1863 Cockerill and Shuttler took three actions in the Brisbane Small Debts Court. These actions were successful but were small in amount and ranged from £1/15/2 to £7/16/2.

The year 1863 was not a good year for Shuttler. He managed to have a legal clash with another butcher. This butcher was the well-known public figure and litigant Patrick Mayne. Shuttler claimed that Alderman Mayne had unlawfully assaulted and beaten him. He argued that Mayne had grabbed him by the beard, pushed, shoved and used threatening language. The Police Magistrate eventually argued that this was a trifling case and should be withdrawn. It was noted in the evidence that Mayne claimed Shuttler owed him 34 sheep.

Shuttler moved to the Toowoomba area and from 1865 was operating a butcher's shop.

The buyer of Lot 2 in October 1870 was Azariah Purchase who was born in Somerset, England 1832. Azariah is a Hebrew name meaning 'helped by God' which suggests that Purchase was Jewish. Azariah Purchase paid what seems a rather low price of £200 for Lot 2.

Prior to purchasing Lot 2, the *Brisbane Courier* contained an advertisement from Duncan and Duncan indicating that, as Azariah Purchase was leaving the city, they would be auctioning:

> his valuable and choicely-situated property in Grey Street, South Brisbane.

It was further stated that Purchase had operated the *Farmers Arms Hotel* on this site and given the size of the building on the site, it could be divided into two comfortable and commodious private houses. No further information was located regarding this auction. Purchase actually held the *Farmers Arms* licence from 1864 to 1869. Surprisingly, in 1869 Purchase wanted to gain a licence for the area known as One-Mile Swamp. This was a water reserve used as a stock resting area for livestock being driven up Logan Road. Purchase apparently owned land and a house at One-Mile Swamp.

From October 1870 when Azariah Purchase obtained Lot 2, there were several legal documents issued regarding the allotment. Perhaps the most important was signed on 7 August 1871, when Purchase entered into a mortgage agreement with Ernest Goertz for £100. The next month on 15 September 1871, Judge Alfred Lutwyche confirmed that Azariah Purchase be adjudged insolvent and that William Henry Miskin be the official assignee in matters relating to his estate. Ernest Goertz was a wine and spirits merchant in Queen Street, and in a mortgage agreement with Purchase, he initially advanced him £100 with Lot 2 as the security. By the time Lutwyche declared that Purchase was insolvent, the amount owing to Goertz was £377 9s 4d. Goertz did own other land in the Moreton Bay District.

The solicitor William Miskin was appointed to manage the estate of Purchase in a manner that would assist creditors. In addition to his legal work, Miskin was a prominent and well-published entomologist, specialising in butterflies. He had an interest in a sugar plantation at Bundall, became Mayor of Toowong and for two years was President of the Queensland branch of the Royal Geographical Society of Australia.[20]

Miskin sold up the stock and property of Azariah Purchase. According to *The Week* in December 1894, Miskin left South Brisbane and returned to Sydney as his wife had successfully petitioned the Supreme Court for dissolution of marriage on the grounds of adultery and desertion.

During the legal process surrounding Lot 2, the opportunity arose for interested parties to make a bid on the allotment. The highest bid was made by Francis Murray who was described as a cabinetmaker, upholsterer, undertaker and money lender. He owned shares in a mining company and had a store in Queen Street. From 1867 to 1872 Murray was an alderman of Brisbane city and was elected mayor in 1871. He died at age 37 years and was buried in Paddington cemetery.

Lot 2 was sold again on 27 March 1872 to George Booth. The sellers were Ernest Goertz and William Henry Miskin, but these were directed by Francis Murray. In the sale documents, Booth was described as a drayman. Lot 2 was the ideal location for a drayman to operate from. It was close to major roads, the docks, ferries and a bridge. Booth made appearances in the Petty Debts and Police Magistrate courts as a number of people were taken to court for small amounts for 'work done by Booth'. It is probable that Booth operated several drays. He had other commercial interests, one being a profitable horse and cab service in the expanding Brisbane.

The *North Australian* newspaper in November 1863 noted that a Mr Booth was the landlord of a house of 'ill fame' in Harcourt Street, South Brisbane. This activity was run by two well-known 'business' women around the South Brisbane inns, Susan Frisbee and her associate, Mary Anne Williams. In a case against this enterprise, the arresting officer Sergeant Maloney said there was a 'constant repetition of debauchery'. Another witness, James Miller, who lived 100 yards from the house concerned, spoke to Mr Booth about the nightly disturbances at the house. A third witness, George Critchlow, claimed that his house was separated from the Booth owned house by a single wall. Critchlow reported that beds had to be moved as far as possible from the wall adjoining the Booth house. Apparently, there was something missing in the evidence, and the magistrates ruled that the case was not fully proved and it was dismissed through a lack of evidence.[21]

It is worth noting that the above mentioned Mary Anne Williams had been practising her skills in South Brisbane for many years. The 'Booth incident' occurred in 1863 but previously in February 1848, the *Moreton Bay Courier* indicated that Mary Anne had been sentenced under the Vagrancy Act and imprisoned in Sydney for two months. In that particular incident, the sentence arose because of her wanderings through the public houses of South Brisbane demonstrating her extensive knowledge of offensive foul language.

In September 1876 the *Queensland Times, Ipswich Herald and General Advertiser* reported the death of J S Booth, described as a drayman from Harcourt Street in South Brisbane. There is no doubt this is George Booth, the owner of the house of ill fame in Harcourt Street. The newspaper notes that this drayman was well-known in Brisbane. Apparently Booth had delivered a load of powder to Ipswich. This powder would have been gunpowder, which for many years was used as a blasting agent. Booth had stopped at the well-known *Drysdale's Hotel,* Goodna, on the way back to South Brisbane, and it was assumed that he had a few drinks. On leaving Goodna, he was standing up in the dray and was jerked out on to the road and killed when the dray ran over him.

### *Title Deed Changes – Lot 2*

| | |
|---|---|
| 1843 | Andrew Graham |
| 1870 | Azariah Purchase |
| 1871 | Ernest Goertz, William Miskin and Francis Murray[NB] |
| 1872 | George Booth |

[NB] Ernest Goertz was owed money. William Miskin, official assignee of the insolvent Purchase and Murray, put in a successful lot bid during the insolvency case.

## Lot 3 William Sheehan

Sheehan initially purchased Lot 3 for £23/2/- and probably did not put any improvements on the allotment before he sold it to James Ramsay on 1 November 1848. Ramsay, a police constable who lived in South Brisbane, paid £33/10/- for the allotment. Whether James and Bridget Ramsay lived in Stanley Street is not known, as he resigned from the Brisbane police on 14 September 1849.

On Saturday 17 September 1929, the *Brisbane Courier* reported a complex court case involving Johanna (Johanna Finucane), the 79-year-old daughter of William Sheehan, the original owner of the allotment. Johanna stated that the Sheehans had initially lived in Woodleigh Cottage on Elizabeth Street, which was between Edward Street and the river. Johanna spoke of her father William as periodically going to Sydney and of riding his horse out to Ipswich. She described William as:

> a wonderful successful man... and the owner of many valuable properties in the city and suburbs... we lived in the lap of luxury. (p.16)

12. St Patricks Tavern, Brisbane, ca 1873. William Sheehan last held the St Patricks licence in 1851. How much did the building change in 22 years?

Johanna commented that when they left *Woodleigh Cottage*, they moved to Milton where her father built a room described as 'a ballroom' onto the house.

In June 1934 the *Courier Mail* reported that there had been some discussion about *St Patricks Tavern*, North Brisbane, and gained the following information from Professor Cumbrae-Stewart. William Sheehan was an innkeeper who held the licence for *St Patricks Tavern* in 1847, 1848 and 1849. In 1850 the licence was held by Mathew Stewart, but Sheehan again held the licence in 1851. Sheehan was refused the licence in 1853, but following some improvements to the tavern, it was granted to Jeremiah Scanlon.

The purchase of Lot 3 by William Sheehan was not his only allotment purchase in Brisbane. An examination of *Ham's Map of the City of Brisbane* (1863) indicates that Sheehan had actually purchased another 21 Lots. These purchases suggest Sheehan had access to considerable financial resources. It is also highly likely that he was a speculative investor.

Initially, it seemed that the Sheehans lived at *St Patricks Tavern*. This may be incorrect as *Woodleigh Cottage* was relatively close to *St Patricks Tavern* in Queen Street. By 1847 he appeared to be spending some time at *Milton Cottage* and eventually moved to this location. This address appears in newspapers a few times but its precise location has not been identified—except that it was in Milton and had stables. The electoral lists indicate that by 1856 Sheehan owned a property in Sandgate and thus became entitled to vote in local elections.

Archival records provide evidence that Sheehan was involved in a considerable amount of litigation. For example, in 1846 he charged Allen and Pittman with having assaulting him at the tavern, and in 1858 there was a case involving a pump, and it was claimed that he had been assaulted by William Taylor. In 1848 there was a claim made by Patrick Pacey that Sheehan had stolen cattle. This case was dismissed. In 1849 Mrs Sheehan was at *St Patricks Inn*, and according to evidence given at the Police Court, was 'grossly attacked' by a drunk named Jeremiah Mahony who threatened to do the same thing to Patrick Sheehan. The court decided that Mahony should pay a fine of £5 or be imprisoned in a Sydney goal for two months.

There were a few cases where Sheehan experienced staff difficulties; the most interesting involved John E Crutchfield. This 1847 case was lodged by George Further, an innkeeper of Ipswich, under the Hired Servants Act. George Further argued that Sheehan had hired his cook 'an African named Crutchfield' without an appropriate written discharge. John Ocock appeared for Sheehan, but Crutchfield 'prevaricated so grossly during his evidence' that he was sent immediately to the cells for 24 hours. Sometime later, Crutchfield made another appearance in court, but by then he had been employed by Sheehan. This reappearance apparently took some time and there was much merriment in court owing to the vehemence and knowledge of bush law displayed by Crutchfield. It was ruled that Sheehan owed Crutchfield £1 17s 8d and that the employment agreement should be cancelled.

In December 1847 the Loyal Brisbane Lodge of the Australian Order of Odd Fellows was opened in Brisbane. The opening function was held at *St Patricks Tavern* with the agreement of Brother William Sheehan. The opening was performed by Brother Henry Palmer Dowse, and he was assisted by Brother John Allen, the commander of the *Tamar*. The chair for the evening was Brother A S Lyon. Dowse, Allen, and Lyon, like Sheehan, were well known identities in early Brisbane.

While Sheehan owned *Milton Cottage*, he certainly made money from having stallions stand at stud in his stables. During the 1840s and for the next 20 years or so, horses were essential in terms of visiting others, shopping and even going to work. Most of the stations on the Darling Downs had a stud horse available to service mares. William Sheehan, in the small but growing Brisbane suburbs, had a horse standing at stud in the stables at *Milton Cottage*. The horses were named and the costs involved were advertised by Sheehan in 1847, 1858 and 1859. If this was a good money earner, it seems likely he would have made available a stud horse in all the years he owned *Milton Cottage*. Sheehan was a businessman and his stud horses were draught horses. Draught horses were essential to the developing areas in northern NSW. They could work on road construction, at the wharves, in the timber and coal industries, and were vital in wagon work around the city. The two stud draught horses used by Sheehan were named Glazer and Tommy; both were well known in Brisbane. The costs involved in servicing a mare were £3 plus 5/- for the assistance of a groom. Stud horses were usually kept at one site. In Sheehan's opinion, this was not the best way to utilise his stud horse assets. Sheehan had the studs at *Milton Cottage* on specific days, and then they were at Eagle Farm on other days. The stud horses also spent some time at John McGrath's. This was probably at Moggill. John and Darby McGrath, both ex-convicts, held land at Moggill from 1848.

William Sheehan had experienced a long period of illness before dying at his Wickham Street home during October 1866. His son, William John Sheehan, was the major benefactor of his will. Sheehan (Jnr) received a thorough education and became a popular young man and a distinguished cricketer. Tragedy struck when he died in a drowning accident near Redcliffe Point. This boating and probable fishing trip involved William J Sheehan, Herbert Slaughter, Llewellyn Best and the two young sons of Edward J Bulmore. The Bulmore boys were not initially on the trip but had waded out to the boat when it was close to shore; sought, and gained permission to go on the trip.

It is believed that a squall tipped the boat over on the way back to Sandgate; all on-board, except Llewellyn Best, lost their lives.

The *Brisbane Courier* and the *Rockhampton Bulletin* contained obituaries. As a consequence of the Rockhampton journalist knowing W J Sheehan from childhood, this article contained more personal insights regarding the deceased man's life. (*Rockhampton Bulletin*, 22 November, 1881. p.3)

> At his father's death he inherited valuable property worth at least £1000 a year ... he fell gradually into a circle of "turfites" and "sharpers" who ... ruined him ... property was sold to pay his debts.

A few days after the tragic accident, reports indicated that the boating party had stopped at *Scarborough Hotel* for about two hours and there were queries regarding the sobriety levels aboard the boat.

The early inns were meeting, drinking and sometimes eating places in South Brisbane. By law, these inns also provided some accommodation. Each of these inns probably had its own special incident over the years. The following is an account of one such incident reported in the *Moreton Bay Courier* about *St Patricks Tavern* in July 1858 when a John Jones held the licence.

In July 1858 it was reported that the proprietor of *St Patricks Tavern*, John Jones, had laid a charge in the Police Court against Eliza, an Indigenous woman, for illegally being on his property. The magistrate, W A Duncan, a highly respected early settler, dismissed the charge. The newspaper described this in a manner and terminology that would now be considered completely inappropriate and discriminatory. Perceptions and attitudes do change, but slowly. It was stated that at 12 o'clock, Eliza, a black gin, was found in bed with the proprietor's negro cook, who was also a ticket-of-leave man. She was sent away but returned at 2 pm. The charge was dismissed.

The Ramsay purchase in 1848 was the only change of title deed supplied by the Titles Office. However, in

13. Schedule for Lot 3 from the office of the Registrar of Titles

1887 Anne Stephens, a widow from Brisbane requested a search of the files regarding Lot 3. Arthur William Praeger, the clerk from the office of the Registrar of Titles replied that there were no encumbrances on the title and supplied a schedule of the legal documents relating to Lot 3. These commenced with William Sheehan from 30 May 1848 and continued until Anne Stephens made the legal request regarding encumbrances in 1897.

It was reported earlier that the title deeds suggested that Sheehan simply sold Lot 3 to James Ramsay in 1848. The schedule provided by Praeger recorded that there were five legal transactions involving James Ramsay and Lot 3. Ramsay was involved in a conveyance with William Sheehan, a mortgage with Sheehan, a reconveyance with Sheehan and a mortgage with Joseph Thompson. The schedule reported a sale of Lot 3 to Thomas Blacket Stephens. Unfortunately, there are no dates in the schedule. Legal actions recorded in the schedule refer to volume and page references in an official Register Book.

The names and organisations appearing on the schedule supplied for Lot 3 were: William Sheehan, James Ramsay, John O'Neil Brenan, Joseph Thompson, Thomas Blacket Stephens, Moreton Bay Building and Investment Society, James Swan, William Thornton, Anne Stephens and Australian Joint Savings Bank Limited.

Some of the names on this schedule were well known with regard to the early history of South Brisbane and Brisbane generally. Sheehan was a businessman and innkeeper in North Brisbane who sold Lot 3 to James Ramsay, a policeman. The next name on the schedule was John O'Neil Brenan who was the NSW Sheriff from 1850 to 1860. There are a number of comments in the literature about Brenan being a difficult man to deal with. When J S Kerr wrote his book on the history of the Parramatta Correctional Centre in 1895, he provided a description of Brenan. Kerr assessed Brenan as a cranky and idiosyncratic man who had 'an even more cranky and idiosyncratic father' (p.14). Irrespective of the seemingly complex attributes of Brenan, it is assumed that a dispute of some nature had arisen relating to Lot 3 and Brenan determined the Lot should be sold to Thomas Blacket Stephens.

T B Stephens from Rochdale in Lancashire was already a wealthy man on his arrival in Moreton Bay District in

1853. He was elected an alderman in 1859 and became the second mayor of Brisbane in 1862. At various times, he was a member of the Legislative Assembly and the Queensland Legislative Council. In 1859 he purchased the *Moreton Bay Courier* and developed this paper through growth stages and name changes, remaining as managing director until 1873.

The next name on the schedule was Thompson. This was most likely Joseph Thompson, but little is known about this person except that the literature describes him as a 'rural entrepreneur' who owned 200 acres between O'Keefe Street and Cockerill's Paddock. The Lot 3 schedule indicates that Thompson and Stephens were involved in a reconveyance.

Stephens next had a legal transaction described as an equity mortgage with James Swan. Swan, born in Glasgow, moved to Sydney travelling with John Dunmore Lang and then on to the Moreton Bay District. In 1846 he worked on the *Moreton Bay Courier* and by 1847 owned the paper. Swan was a successful man, deeply involved in community affairs and a devout Baptist. He became an alderman and then Mayor of Brisbane from 1873-1875.

When Swan's death was reported in 1891 and his will lodged for probate, newspapers stated that the estate was valued at £36,000. Those benefiting from the will were listed as: his wife, £500 per annum; various Churches, £1000 each; Christian Disciple Church, £500; Wharf Street Baptist Church, £500 and the residue was estimated to produce £25000 for the Queensland Baptist Association (Brisbane).

When the Supreme Court examined Swan's will, it was reported that it had only two witnesses and not the required three. In addition, the will had never been registered. As a consequence of these errors, Swan's wife became the sole benefactor of the will. When Swan's wife died in 1930, the estate passed to the Baptist Church for what was described as 'the support of evangelists of impeccable orthodoxy'.

Swan had considerable involvement in property development. An example of this development work was at 678 Ann Street, Fortitude Valley.

14. Suzie Wongs Good Time Bar, 678 Ann Street, Fortitude Valley

Swan constructed this building in the 1870s and leased the space to three small-scale businesses. With the passage of time, there have been some alterations to 678 Ann Street. Swan, a devout Baptist, may have hoped his construction would not become a good time bar.

William Thornton was initially from Ireland, and on arrival in the colony spent some time working in Sydney. In June 1846 the *Moreton Bay Courier* reported that Thornton was arriving in Brisbane on the next trip made by the steamer *Tamar*. He had been appointed landing-waiter and tides surveyor in a new Customs organisation. A landing-waiter supervised the arrival of goods at a docking site. Thornton and his wife lived at Kangaroo Point. Thornton progressed in Customs and became a water police magistrate and when Queensland separated from NSW in 1859, he was appointed the Collector of Customs, a position he held until 1892. In addition, he held a seat in the Legislative Council for 13 years.

The Lot 3 schedule shows that Thornton was involved in a mortgage and release of mortgage with T B Stephens.

In June of 1884 the *Brisbane Courier* contains the obituary for William Thornton, and it is noted that he was a local director of the Australian Joint Savings Bank. No date is provided for this directorship, but it is assumed that it was outside the dates when Thornton was involved as an individual in legal transactions noted for Lot 3.

T B Stephens was involved in a mortgage and release of a mortgage with the Moreton Bay Building and Investment Society. William and Elizabeth Connolly of Lot 1 had dealings with this society where Robert Little, Dr William Hobbs and John Richardson were the trustees; each was a successful man in Moreton Bay.

The lack of financial structures in early Brisbane hindered development. It was not until 1859 that the Bank of New South Wales established a branch in Queen Street. This bank and the Moreton Bay Building and Investment Society, mentioned above, represent the establishment of early banking structures in Brisbane.

The last entry on the schedule is Anne Stephens who paid a mortgage to the Australian Joint Savings Bank Ltd. This bank was initially set up in NSW in 1852, and its agencies were generally located at the discovery of gold sites in NSW. An agency was established at South Brisbane in 1862–63 and it seems highly unlikely that this was related to gold discovery.

Anne Stephens was the widow of Thomas Blacket Stephens who died in 1877. The last entry in the Prager schedule was Anne Stephens who repaid a mortgage held by the Joint Stock Bank Ltd in 1879. Anne Stephens continued to operate part of her late husband's commercial interests, namely the section dealing with fellmongering. This was the trading in hides and skin. (In old English 'fell' could mean skins and 'monger' a dealer.)

### Title Deed Changes – Lot 3

| | |
|---|---|
| 1843 | William Sheehan |
| 1848 | James Ramsay |
| 1870 | Thomas Blacket Stephens |
| 1879 | Anne Stephens |

## Lot 4 William Lacy

William and Margaret Lacy held the initial title to their allotment for longer than any of the five original purchasers considered in this book. William Lacy died 1 September 1874 and Margaret Lacy 13 May 1881, but the tile remained in William's name.

The title package concerning this allotment reports that there had been no changes in the title by 1877 and that a declaration by William Boys resulted in a movement from the old Torrens title system to the 1861 Real Property Act.

William Boys, a Brisbane coal merchant, made his declaration before George Cross JP (16 May 1887). In this document, Boys declared that William Lacy had appointed him (Boys) and Lewis Lacy, William and Mary's son, executors and trustees. Lewis had been a mail contractor at Georgetown, in the Shire of Etheridge, Queensland, but died in 1881.

The declaration went on to indicate that the remaining children in the Lacy family requested that the allotment be sold. Boys suggested that the allotment would bring a better price if it were to be moved under the provisions of the 1861 Real Property Act.

Allotment 4 was moved under the Real Property Act with Boys suggesting that it could be valued at £4000, which seemed an optimistic figure. It was pointed out by Boys that the allotment was currently being leased by the large international firm Alfred Shaw & Co, which had commenced operations in Melbourne but had branches in England, Brisbane and Townsville.

It seemed that as long as Lot 4 was being leased in a satisfactory manner there would be no sale of the land. When the Intercolonial Exhibition was held in Brisbane in 1876, Alfred Shaw and Co had on display a working windmill which supplied water to a number of exhibitors. This event is now considered the first Ekka (Brisbane Exhibition).

## *Title Deed Changes – Lot 4*

| | |
|---|---|
| 1843 | William Lacy |
| 1887 | William Lacy (Leased) |

15. Alfred Shaw & Co, Intercolonial Exhibition, Brisbane 1876

## Lot 5 John Orr

John Orr operated a butcher's shop on Lot 5 for a number of years, and when the title deeds were obtained for the five South Brisbane allotments, Kaye Nardella, the senior curator at Department of Mapping, Natural Resources and Energy made the following comment in an email (17/4/20):

> I could not see a reference to an application packet for the first Torrens system, and it is difficult to see if any of the numbers written on the first freehold title can refer to an application packet.

In other words, the title records tell us little. Newspapers reported that Orr made the original purchase but noted that some other butcher took over from Orr. The *Courier* in September and December 1861 carried advertisements relating to the sale of John Orr's butchery. These advertisements described the new owner, William Baynes, as a 'shipping and family butcher' and indicated that Baynes had taken over the shop of J and W Orr at Stanley Quay, South Brisbane. An immediate change occurred with deliveries of meat by boat to all parts of the river.

Baynes' enterprise expanded rapidly and although Lot 5 remained a butcher's shop for many years, there was further expansion to other sites: first to Queensport where there was a focus on the preservation of meat, and secondly to Belmont where fellmongering, wool scouring and soap making became profitable pursuits.

William Baynes and other family members established The Graziers Butchering Company and the Graziers Meat Exporting Company. In addition to the expansion into export markets, 50 suburban butcher shops were developed by the Grazier's Butchering Company in the city of Brisbane.

## *Title Deed Changes – Lot 5*

| | |
|---|---|
| 1843 | John Orr |
| 1861 | William Baynes |

## Hannah and the Allotments

In 1861 Hannah left the area she knew well, moved to Ipswich and became the licensee of an inn again. She died in 1862.

At this time, the Connollys had sold Lot 1, but they continued to live in the South Brisbane area. Robert Towns was now running part of his business operations from Lot 1.

The Graham's old allotment, Lot 2, was still in the name of Graham and it continued to operate as an inn. It is difficult to be certain as to how the Grahams made decisions relating to the licensees for their two sites. It seems likely that if non-family members wanted to lease the sites that would occur. When Hannah married Frank Mercer and he was interested in becoming an innkeeper, it would have been easy to allocate one of the Graham sites to him. This did not occur. It is assumed that the money obtained from the leased sites was a significant portion of the income for the Graham and Mercer families.

William Sheehan, the initial owner of Lot 3, became a wealthy and well known Brisbane businessman. Hannah had contact with Sheehan for some years after he sold Lot 3. Of all the five initial owners, Hannah probably considered Sheehan a friend.

By the time Hannah died at Ipswich, the lots owned by Lacy (Lot 4) and Orr (Lot 5) were in the process of becoming industrial sites: one being leased by a general merchant from the UK, Alfred Shaw & Co, and the other, a part of William Baynes' international butchery.

## Overview

An examination of ownership based on the changes in title deeds for the five South Brisbane allotments supports the contention that each allotment has a story to tell. In general, commercial ambitions were behind each change in the title of an allotment.

The appeal of these allotments to buyers arose from such factors as access to a navigable river and the periodic bridge link to the Darling Downs. There was also the talk that this area could well become the commercial centre of Brisbane. Floods ended this aspiration. The allotments were linked to a network of rough and boggy streets. Horse-drawn drays, wagons and jinkers used this network to deliver small but essential produce such as bread, milk and meat. The heavy trade of coal, timber, flour and alcohol also made use of the roads.

The navigable river was probably the main draw card, but if you had asked the owners of the five allotments, it would be no surprise if they identified this same river as one of their potential threats.

The following table indicates the names of the initial purchasers in 1843 through to the owners in 1887.

| Year | Lot 1 | Lot 2 | Lot 3 | Lot 4 | Lot 5 |
|---|---|---|---|---|---|
| 1843 | Elizabeth Connolly | Andrew Graham | William Sheehan | William Lacy | John Orr |
| 1848 | | | James Ramsay | | |
| 1851 | John Ocock | | | | |
| 1851 | William Connolly and wife, Elizabeth | | | | |
| 1851 | John McCabe | | | | |
| 1853 | Roger Elliott | | | | |
| 1856 | Robert Towns | | | | |
| 1861 | | | | | William Baynes |
| 1870 | | Azariah Purchase | Thomas Blacket Stephens | | |
| 1871 | | Earnst Goertz, William Miskin and Francis Murray | | | |
| 1872 | | George Booth | | | |
| 1875 | Henry Lock | | | | |
| 1879 | John Hardgrave | | Anne Stephens | | |
| 1887 | | | | William Lacy (Leased) | |

16. Table showing the names of the initial owners of Allotment 1-5, Section 3, South Brisbane, 1843 and the year of title deed changes through to 1887

The initial decision was to examine the title deeds up to 1870. There were a number of interesting transactions after 1870 and it was decided to comment on these when they seemed to provide differing perspectives or greater clarity about life in this area of South Brisbane.

An immense amount of data was collected from the title deeds for the five South Brisbane allotments. The hand written documents ranged in length from two to seventeen pages. It was the style of writing that made the reading of documents demanding, particularly the writing being very small in size, with the words frequently touching and being packed into the lines. A lack of familiarity with early title documents added to the task of interpretation. There were several issues that were deemed the most significant in this analysis. These were the financial challenges involved, complexity of transactions, frequency of allotment sales, expense and length of ownership, public office and purchasing an allotment, and the most unusual buyer.

## *Financial Challenges*

Two buyers failed in, or just after, the process of meeting the purchase requirements. In 1879 Henry Lock (Lot 1) borrowed £900 at 8% interest per annum and was soon experiencing financial difficulties. Azariah Purchase (Lot 2) appears to have had prior success in financial deals. However, within 12 months of purchasing Lot 2 in 1870, he had borrowed money and was declared insolvent.

## Complexity of Transactions

The first change of title in the five allotments occurred in November 1848 when William Sheehan sold Lot 3 to James Ramsay, a policeman. Initially, this had the appearance of the simple sale of an allotment. The Schedule for Lot 3, discussed previously, indicates this sale was quite a legal tangle.

## Frequency of Allotment Sales

Connolly's Lot 1 sold five times by 1870. The ownership of the other allotments was extremely stable. Sheehan's Lot 3 sold 2 times, Graham's Lot 2 sold once, as did Orr's Lot 5. Lacy's Lot 4 was not sold during this period. The corner location of Lot 1 provided a somewhat superior site with respect to the wharfs, river and street access.

## Expense and Length of Ownership

The most expensive purchase of the South Brisbane allotments was made by Henry Lock in 1875. Lock, who had been an innkeeper, paid Robert Towns' trustees of Lot 1, £975. Lock had borrowed £900 of the purchase price.

Lot 2 was initially purchased by Andrew Graham and stayed in the Graham name until 1870. In that period of time, the licence for the inn was in the name of Andrew Graham and then Hannah Graham. When the allotment was sold in October 1870, the ownership group reflected an association of family members. The exception to this was Thomas Shuttler. He may have joined the selling group as a consequence of a prior partnership with John Cockerill, the husband of Annie Graham.

William Lacy owned Lot 4, and this appears to have remained in his name for over 30 years. In 1877 a trustee of Lacy's affairs updated the allotment title. However, the remaining members of the Lacy family decided to continue the lease to the current leaseholder, an international firm.

## International and Local Buyers of Allotments

The best examples of international buyers and lessees were Robert Towns (Towns and Co) Lot 1 and Alfred Shaw and Co (Lot 4). Towns had already established a large business in Sydney before he commenced a branch in Brisbane. His business activities were largely in the Pacific Islands and it was his involvement with Pacific Islanders that damaged his reputation. Towns owned Lot 1 for 19 years.

Lacy's Lot 4 was leased rather than purchased by Alfred Shaw & Co. We know the lease was continued in 1877. This firm commenced in England and had a number of branches in various countries. No documentation was located as to when they first leased, or ceased to lease Lot 4. The hardware sold by this firm was imported from England. Lot 4, with wharfs across the road, was an important site for Alfred Shaw & Co.

As mentioned before, Jacob Montefiore purchased a Connolly allotment a few hundred metres up river from the five allotments considered in this study. He held this allotment for 14½ years. Montefiore had diverse interests in commercial activities and it would not be a surprise if similar types of businessmen arrived during the expansion of South Brisbane.

In terms of local buyers, William Baynes from Toowoomba purchased Orr's butchers shop in 1861 and used this site (Lot 5) as the take-off point for the commencement of an international butchery. Thomas Blacket Stephens arrived in Sydney in 1849 but moved to Brisbane. He became Mayor of Brisbane in 1862 and in 1870 purchased Lot 3. After his death, his wife Anne purchased the same allotment. T B Stephens had been involved in woollen mills in England. He became 'a local' in Brisbane, buying a newspaper, establishing a fellmongering business, and becoming Mayor of Brisbane.

In 1837 James Swan arrived in Sydney with the controversial Presbyterian minister Dr John Dunmore Lang who had a massive involvement in the religious, educational and political debates of early Australia.

Swan moved to Brisbane and was quickly involved in community affairs and investment. He did not purchase one of the allotments, but the Schedule for Lot 3 shows that he was involved in the financing of a buyer for Lot 3. By 1847 he purchased the *Moreton Bay Courier* and in 1873–75 became Mayor of Brisbane. Swan did purchase a great deal of Brisbane real estate, which included two suburban hotels. Both Stephens and Swan were ardent Baptists and in such a small population, obviously knew each other.

## *Public Office and Purchasing an Allotment*

A number of years after these allotments were taken up, various mayors of Brisbane purchased one of these five allotments. Thomas Blacket Stephens was Mayor in

1862, and he purchased Lot 3 in 1870. In 1871 Francis Murray was Mayor, and in the same year was involved in a joint ownership of Lot 2. John Hardgrave was Mayor in 1868–69, and ten years later purchased Lot 2. James Swan, Mayor 1873–75, did not own Lot 3, but made a loan available to a purchaser of that Lot. In 1880 William Henry Miskin was the first president of the Shire of Toowong, and in 1871 he was a joint owner of Lot 2.

## *Most Unusual Buyer of an Allotment*

Lot 2 had a history of being an inn. In 1872 Lot 2 was purchased by George Booth, who was described as a drayman. The initial image was of a scruffy man with an aged horse and weathered dray—perhaps similar to the main character in 'Steptoe and Son', the 1960s–70s British TV show. This may be a distorted image. He probably had several drays operating from the wharfs which were less than 100 metres away. He was certainly operating at least one horse and cab in the city. George Booth owned a house of ill repute in Harcourt Street. Even Booth's death in 1875 was unusual. He fell out of his horse-drawn wagon: it ran over him and he was killed.

## Conclusions and Hannah's Views

Although Hannah had died in 1862, in these conclusions the liberty has been taken to voice her possible views as to what had occurred in the five South Brisbane allotments.

By 1870 four of the five allotments had experienced change and development. This did not apply to Graham's Lot 2 as family owners kept it as a small inn, or leased it as an inn. It is highly likely that Hannah would be extremely pleased that Lot 2, 'her lot', remained a small inn in the name of Andrew Graham, her first husband. Orr's Lot 5 continued in the meat business but moved from a family operation to a national, and then international operation under William Baynes. Hannah could well have accepted the notion of Baynes delivering meat to locals along the river but going 'international' meant massive change and Hannah may have struggled with such an outcome.

Connolly's Lot 1 sold five times by 1870 and the highest selling price was £975. Such outcomes were most likely related to the advantages arising from the physical location of the allotment. Elliott's purchase of this allotment was based on his financial success as a whaler, and Towns came to South Brisbane as an established businessman. Robert Towns and Co paid cash for Lot 1, and Alfred Shaw and Co held a lease for Lot 4. The decision to lease or pay cash would have been dependent on both the financial standing and potential objectives of the parties involved in the transactions. It is questionable whether Hannah would have appreciated such large international businesses as those owned by Towns and Shaw obtaining a foothold in 'her part' of South Brisbane. She was probably aware of the danger that 'small cogs' can be crushed when the 'big wheels' move in.

There were local business persons who purchased allotments. These included T B Stephens and his wife Anne, who both held Lot 3 at different dates. Hannah may have wondered how the Stephens had so much money, but as they stayed on as locals, she may have grudgingly accepted them. When Stephens purchased the local newspaper, she would have realised he was an influential 'big wheel' in the locality. Booth, the drayman who held Lot 2, would have been viewed as a local businessman, and Hannah would have totally accepted a 'local horse and drayman' as an allotment owner. She would also have known that he drank at local inns and was thus a potential customer. Having owned and managed an inn in a rough part of the colony, Hannah was probably not a 'shrinking violet'. It is possible she shrugged her shoulders when mention was made of Booth's brothel. She was probably 'staggered' when she heard that someone was contemplating borrowing £900 to buy an inn. Her husband, Andrew, paid £29/14/- for his allotment in 1842.

John Ocock, the lawyer, clearly had some financial dealings with the Connollys (Lot 1). James Swan and William Thornton had financial involvement with Sheehan's Lot 3. Charles Watson, about whom nothing was located, was able to make a loan to Henry Lock of £900 for Lot 1. James Swan and T B Stephens knew each other well and both were devout Baptists. The schedule of legal documents for Lot 3, requested by Anne Stephens, indicates that these two had dealings relating to a mortgage involved in the purchase of this Lot. The Swan-Stephens business association was also evident in 1859 when Swan sold the *Moreton Bay Courier* to T B Stephens. This was the only example located suggesting the possibility that friendship and religious faith may have been evident in the sale of the analysed allotments. Hannah would have recognised the importance of friendship in an isolated and potentially dangerous community. On the other hand, it is difficult to know where she stood on religion. She would have known that religion had the capacity to both unite and divide a community. It is highly likely she knew that religious debate would lead to trouble in her inn.

The formal banking structures were slow to develop in South Brisbane, but there was some mention of the Moreton Bay Building and Investment Society, Australian Joint Savings Bank and the Bank of NSW.

## Hannah & Friends: Life in South Brisbane

The early colonists were somewhat suspicious of banks, but given the amount of cash floating around in an inn, it is possible that Hannah grudgingly put money in the bank.

A difficult question to answer is—would other samples of allotments in early South Brisbane produce similar results to those in Stanley Street? If they were on the river and near a wharf, the answer is probably yes. Those buying away from the river may well have been influenced by proximity to a particular church or school. As in most areas, the price of land would be a significant factor for those choosing South Brisbane as a home or business site. There would also be buyers whose decision would be strongly influenced by the potential for future financial gain.

There was evidence of the large 'outsider' businesses, such as Robert Towns and Alfred Shaw, moving into South Brisbane. It was, however, 'the locals' such as William Sheehan, John McCabe and George Booth who added the personal character to the area. At various times each of these locals lived relatively close to Hannah. It is clear that William Sheehan and Hannah were friends over a period of years. McCabe and Hannah were innkeepers located less than a 2–3 minute walk from each other in a relatively low population area. They would have definitely known each other. When the sailing ships tied up in South Brisbane, George Booth operated his horse and dray business virtually in Hannah's house yard; he may have had an occasional beer at her inn. After many months at sea, some of the crew from the sailing ships may have obtained directions to another of George's businesses.

Sheehan with his 21 allotments, horse studs and innkeeper activities, reportedly lived a life of luxury. McCabe, although described as an innkeeper, was also an investor. He may well have been the only early South Brisbane settler who had a dog shot by a local and a horse stabbed to death, probably by a local. George Booth, the successful drayman and Harcourt Street brothel owner, was certainly one of the few South Brisbanites run over and killed by their own wagon.

17. This present-day (2019) aerial photograph of South Brisbane shows the original location of the two lots owned by Andrew Graham—where Hannah lived and was an innkeeper.

What would Hannah have made of
the South Brisbane of today?

# Endnotes

## Part 1

1. Perez, Caroline. (2019), *Invisible Women: Data Bias in a World Designed by Men*, Vintage Arrow.

2. Hansford, Brian. (2016), *The Elusive Archibald Young: Tracing His Footprints in the Moreton Bay District 1844–1875*, Boolarong Press, Brisbane. Hansford, Brian. (2018), *William Jubb: From Promise to Disaster: Darling Downs 1845–1878*, Inspire Point Publishing, Beenleigh.

3. *Moreton Bay Courier*, 28 April 1855, p.3.

4. Rushen, Elizabeth. (2014), *Colonial Duchesses: The migration of Irish women to New South Wales before the Great Famine*, Anchor Books, Sydney.

5. The Australian Agricultural Company was formed in London in 1824 and given the right to take up 1,000,000 acres and their mineral rights. This company spread along rivers in NSW and then moved into Queensland.

6. *Descendants of James Orr (1793-1935)—Roots Web,* (pp.32). Ebenezer Orr had been at Boyd Town as postmaster and a storeman. In 1844 he held the licence for the *Sea Horse* and *Steam Packet Hotel* in Boyd Town, Broulee. He moved from Boyd Town to Moreton Bay. In March 1846 Orr was a signatory to a letter to the Colonial Secretary about the need to establish a Post Office in South Brisbane and another letter concerning the opening of a spring near Ferry Road to supply water for the township of South Brisbane. In February he wrote to the Surveyor General in Sydney requesting 50 acres at 'The Springs near Cunningham Gap', a request that was refused. He also managed runs on the Logan River. By 1862 Ebenezer and James Orr were made magistrates at Coonabarabran and by 1868 Ebenezer had moved his head station to Garrawilla Station. The *Australian Town and Country Journal* 10 January 1874 reported that the Orr brothers sold Garrawilla, their head station and 11 large nearby runs.

   It should be noted that Ebenezer and James Orr at some stage received financial assistance from their brother-in-law Robert Campbell (1811-1887) an enormously successful merchant and land owner, (*The Family of James Orr of St Aubyn's, Hove*).

7. *Moreton Bay Courier*, 23 October 1847, p.3.

8. Morrison, A.A. (1962), *Brisbane One Hundred Years Ago*. Paper read to the Royal Historical Society of Queensland, 25 October 1962.

9. Fisher, R. (2012), *The Best of Colonial Brisbane*. Salisbury: Boolarong Press. p.126.

10. Fisher, R. (2012), *The Best of Colonial Brisbane*. Salisbury: Boolarong Press. p.4.

11. Norris, Merle. (1993), *Brisbane Hotels and Publicans Index 1942-1900*, Brisbane History Group, Series No.6.

12. Wickham's letters are reported on various websites. There is a good account of the Fortitude incident in Chapter 5 of *Brisbane: Schemes and Dreams: Nineteenth Century Arrivals*. (2014). Eds. Harrison, J & Shaw B. Boolarong Press, Queensland.

## Part 2

13. As Brisbane's town plan developed, Stanley Street's location of the 1840s largely disappeared and is now adjacent to the Woolloongabba Cricket Ground. *Ham's Map of the City of Brisbane* (1863) contains the location of the 5 allotments in Section 3, and allotment 5, Section 6, South Brisbane. The image of the map was obtained from museum@dnrme.qld.gov.au.

14. Information relating to the title deeds for the specific South Brisbane allotments was obtained from CSE@dnrme.qld.gov.au (Department of Natural Resources, Mines and Energy).

15. *Queenslander*, 13 March 1915, p.8.

16. B*risbane Courier*, 27 April 1918, p.15.

17. Nehemiah Bartley. (1896), *Australian Pioneers and Reminiscences*, Ed J J Knight, Brisbane, Gordon and Gotch, p.250.

18. See http://www.brisbanehistory.com, Paddington cemetery, p.13.

19. *Huxtables Ballarat Directory*, 1858, p.64.

20. *Encyclopaedia of Australian Science*, Miskin, William Henry (1842-1913).

21. *North Australian*, 12 November, 1863, p.2.

## *Index of People*

Alford, Thomas, 95
Archer, Thomas, 142
Ballow, David, 46
Banbury, Robert, 67
Bartley, Nehemiah, 79, 95, 105-6, 111, 143, 148, 209
Baxter, William, 98
Baynes, William, 120, 122, 187-88, 190, 192, 196, 198
Bennett, James, 31, 144
Berkman, Marcus, 93
Bigge, Francis, 47
Booth, George, 168-70, 192, 197, 199, 201-2
Boys, William, 121-2, 184-5
Bracker, Fred, 41-2, 72
Brenan, John O'Neil, 179
Brown, William, 150
Bulmore, Edward, 176
Burns, Garrick, 91
Burns, James, 99
Cadell, Thomas, 44, 54
Campbell, John, 47, 151
Campbell, Robert, 207
Cash, James, 33-4
Chambers, T, 103

Champoo, 90-1, 120
Chubb, Charles, 105
Clark, William, 142
Cockerill, Annie, 164-5, 194
Cockerill, John, 113, 159, 164-5, 180, 194
Cockle, James, 111
Coley, Richard, 47, 66
Collins, John, 48
Collins, Thomas, 47
Connolly, Elizabeth, 139, 141, 145-6, 149-50, 158-9, 182
Connolly, John, 44
Connolly, William, 145-6, 149, 153, 155, 158-9, 161-2, 182, 189, 194-5, 198, 200
Crawford, Joseph, 147
Critchlow, George, 169
Croft, George, 35-7, 71, 128
Cross, George, 184
Cumbrae-Stewart, Frank, 25, 173
Davidson, Robert, 47
Davies, John, 161-2
Day, John, 33
Denham, Thomas, 98-9
Dickinson, John, 102
Diggles, Sylvester, 113
Dix, Robert, 26, 93
Donivan, Daniel, 113
Dowse, Henry, 175
Dowse, Thomas, 27, 51, 161
Drowden, George, 108
Duncan, William, 83, 166, 178
Elliott, Roger, 150, 152-3, 158, 199
Ferriter, John, 83
Finucane, Johanna, 171
Frisbee, Susan, 169

Fitzgerald, James, 100-1
Fitzpatrick, Mary Anne, 21,122
Fitzpatrick, William, 21-2, 67-8, 122
FitzRoy, Charles, 32, 145, 163
Frawley, Martin, 51, 54
Friend, Thomas, 83
Gill, Francis, 162
Glennie, Benjamin, 47, 66-7
Goertz, Ernest, 167-8, 170, 192
Goode, Catherine, 150
Gorry, Christopher, 109-10
Graham, Andrew, ix, 8, 10, 13-25, 28, 30, 33-39, 44-47, 50, 52, 60-1, 65-68, 73, 82, 95, 97, 110-3, 117-9, 121, 125-9, 131, 134, 141, 163-5, 170, 192, 194, 198, 200, 204
Graham, Andrew (Jnr), 110, 126
Graham, Annie (Ann), 14-6, 20, 30, 66, 100-2, 111-9, 141, 164-5, 194
Graham, Catherine, 15-20, 66, 163-5
Graham, George, 16
Graham, Hannah, vii-xi, 2-4, 7-13, 16-7, 19-21, 25, 28, 30-3, 35, 37, 42, 45-6, 50-1, 53, 58, 61, 64-9, 73-7, 80-2, 85-6, 89-91, 95-135, 141, 164-5, 189-90, 194, 198-204
Graham, John, 30, 98, 110, 112, 119, 126, 164
Graham, John (Rev), 13-4, 20, 161, 163
Graham, Richard, 30 110,126
Graham, Richard (uncle), 13
Graham, Selina, 34, 118
Graham, Thomas, 14, 16-7
Graham, Robert, 159
Gray, Charles, 87-8
Gray, Walter, 47
Grenier, Mary, 148
Grenier, Thomas, 58, 148
Greenwood, Christopher, 123

Greenwood, Edward, 123
Greenwood, James, 123
Greenwood, Mary, 123
Greenwood, Sarah, 100, 123
Gregor, John, 46
Hanly, James, 20
Hardgrave, John, 157, 192, 197
Harney, Jeremiah, 100-3, 119, 123, 128-9, 135
Harrison, J, 208
Hassler, Henri, 111-3
Herden, William, 106, 109-10
Hobbs, William, 149,183
Holden, George, 67
Jubb, Margaret, 7, 32, 118
Jubb, William, vii, 9, 32, 48, 206
Jones, John, 178
Kerr, James, 179
Knight, John, 36-7, 209
Knox, Catherine, 10, 13-4, 163
Knox, Edward, 157
Lacy, John, 121
Lacy, Lewis, 121, 184
Lacy, Margaret, 121, 184
Lacy, William, 23, 64, 121, 141, 184-5, 190, 192, 194-5
Lang, Dunmore, 40, 60, 77, 98, 129, 152, 180, 196
Leonard, John, 33
Lilley, Charles, 101, 124
Little, Robert, 46, 67-8, 149, 183
Lock, Henry, 155-8, 192-4, 200
Lutwyche, Alfred, 91, 99, 101-2, 167
Lyon, Arthur, 85-6, 124, 128, 134,175
Lyons, William, 25
Macintyre, John, 47
Mackenzie, Colin, 47

McCabe, John, 58, 84, 119, 122-3, 146-51, 158, 192, 201-2
McCarthy, William, 67
McGrath, Darby, 82, 176
McGrath, John, 176
McMahon, John, 76
Maloney, Thomas, 169
Mayne, Patrick, 71, 92, 166
Melton, Chas, 143
Mehan, James, 105
Melville, John, 97-8, 123, 135
Melville, William, 58, 96, 98, 123, 135
Miller, Eliza L, 152
Miller, James, 169
Miskin, William, 167-8, 170, 192, 197, 209
Montefiore, Jacob, xi, 159-62, 195
Mort, Henry, 87-8
Murray, Francis, 168, 170, 196-7, 192
Ocock, John, 119, 146, 158-9, 174, 200
Orr, Ebenezer, ix, 26-7, 207
Orr, G, 165
Orr, James, 26, 207
Orr, Jessica, 46, 76, 119
Orr, John, 21, 26, 45-6, 55, 58, 64, 90-91, 119-20, 122, 141, 143, 165, 187-88, 190, 192, 194, 196, 198
Orr, J & W, 120, 165, 187
Peterson, Daniel, 47
Phelan, Richard, 161, 167
Praeger, Arthur, 178
Purchase, Azariah, 164, 166-8, 170, 192-3
Ramsay, Bridget, 171
Ramsay, James, 171, 178-9, 183, 192, 194
Richardson, John, 46, 149, 183
Rolleston, Christopher, 47, 72

Scanlon, Jerimah, 173
Shaw, Alfred, xii, 185, 190, 195, 199, 201
Sheehan, William, 141, 143, 171, 173-79, 183, 190, 194, 200-2
Sheehan, William (Jnr), 176
Shuttler, Thomas, 164-6, 194
Simpson, Stephen, 47, 51
Slaughter, Herbert, 176
Smith, John, 47
Smith, Richard, 40, 47, 87-8
Smith, Teresa, 115
Stephens, Thomas, 179, 182-3, 192, 196, 199-200
Stephens, Anne, 178-9, 183, 192, 196, 199-200
Stewart, Mathew, 173
Stuart, Alexander, 153, 157
Swan, James, 179-82, 196-7, 200
Thompson, Joseph, 178-80
Thornton, William, 82, 179,182, 200
Towns, Robert, 153-8, 162, 189, 192, 194-5, 199-200
Towns, Sophie, 157
Watson, Charles, 157, 200
Way, David, 147
Wentworth, D'Arcy, 157
Wentworth, William, 157
Wickham, John, 3, 22, 46, 68, 81, 83, 87, 129, 143, 208
Young, Archibald, vii, 9, 87, 92, 206